Aspects of modern soc

The social structure of

GENERAL EDITORS

John Barron Mays
Eleanor Rathbone Professor of Social Science, University of Liverpool

Maurice Craft
Goldsmiths' Professor of Education, University of London

The Mass Media

Peter Golding B.Sc., M.A.

Research Officer
Centre for Mass Communication Research
University of Leicester

Longman

Longman Group Limited
Longman House, Burnt Mill, Harlow
Essex CM20 2JE, England
Associated companies throughout the world

*Published in the United States of America
by Longman Inc., New York*

© Longman Group Limited 1974

First published 1974
Sixth impression 1984

ISBN 0582 48116.3 paper

Library of Congress Catalogue Card Number 73.94317

Set in Baskerville

Printed in Singapore by
The Print House Pte Ltd

Editors' Preface

British higher education is now witnessing a very rapid expansion of teaching and research in the social sciences, and, in particular, in sociology. This new series has been designed for courses offered by universities, colleges of education, colleges of technology, and colleges of further education to meet the needs of students training for social work, teaching and a wide variety of other professions. It does not attempt a comprehensive treatment of the whole field of sociology, but concentrates on the social structure of modern Britain which forms a central feature of most university and college sociology courses in this country. Its purpose is to offer an analysis of our contemporary society through the study of basic demographic, ideological and structural features, and through the study of such major social institutions as the family, education, the economic and political structure, and so on.

The aim has been to produce a series of introductory texts which will in combination form the basis for a sustained course of study, but each volume has been designed as a single whole and can be read in its own right.

We hope that the topics covered in the series will prove attractive to a wide reading public and that, in addition to students, others who wish to know more than is readily available about the nature and structure of their own society will find them of interest.

JOHN BARRON MAYS
MAURICE CRAFT

Foreword

No substantial work on the sociology of the mass media in Britain could be written without extensive use of the output of the Centre for Mass Communication Research at Leicester University. My debt to the Centre's Director, Professor Halloran, and to other colleagues there is amply apparent throughout this book. I am particularly grateful to Paul Croll, Richard Dembo, Liz Eyre-Brook, Guy Phelps and Adrian Wells for the opportunity to use unpublished research. Shen Colman, Paul Croll and Graham Murdock all made very helpful comments on the manuscript, not all of which were ignored. To Jean Goddard, Winifred Jefferson and Enid Nightingale my grateful thanks for their efficient production of the typescript.

PETER GOLDING

Acknowledgements

We are grateful to the following for permission to reproduce copyright material:
The Advertising Association for the table 'Distribution of Advertising by Media' by R. A. Critchley from *Advertising Quarterly,* summer 1973; Her Majesty's Stationery Office for data from *Family Expenditure Survey 1971* and Merlin Press Limited for 2 tables from 'The Political Economy of Mass Communications' by Murdock and Golding from *Socialist Register 1973* edited by R. Miliband and J. Saville.

Contents

The mass media and social science   1

Concern about the various mass media far preceded any interest taken in them by the social sciences. Prewar social scientific research on mass communications in Britain is virtually non-existent, and it is only with the emergence of anxiety about the effects of television in the last fifteen years or so that sociology has entered the debate. This book is concerned with the media organisations themselves, and the ways sociologists can understand their history, structure and social constitutions. Such a review of Britain's media is frustrated by the lack of relevant research. This introductory chapter examines the way systematic knowledge of the sociology of Britain's media has been retarded and moulded by public debate about their effects.

Many of the moral and social concerns now expressed about television reflect a long pedigree stretching back at least to political fears about the potency of the popular radical Press in the early nineteenth century, and to critical dismay over the cruder vulgarities of a great deal of mass entertainment in the age of industrialisation. Belief in the persuasiveness of the media, in their moral impact, monopolisation of leisure and erosion of traditional pursuits, intellectual frivolousness and triviality, has not only shaped the way the media behave, but has also had enormous impact on the questions addressed by critics and social scientists. Not surprisingly many large areas of ignorance remain, while shoals of red herrings have nurtured a great deal of unimportant research and uninformed criticism which hinder our understanding of the media in contemporary Britain. A

1

brief look at the source of these misunderstandings is a fruitful introduction to the relationship between the media and society.

THE MEDIA AND SOCIAL CONCERN

Rapid technological changes bring in their wake unease as to the effects of such changes and much criticism of their impact on traditional ways of life. Not surprisingly the more innovatory media have been tarred with the same condemnatory brush. One early critic of television, for example, felt that

> Into this feverish world of atomic bombs balanced so perilously between peace and war, has come a new menace, the menace of television — Jekyll and Hyde of the atom . . . a force capable of bringing a revolution to culture and entertainment, yet at the same time repulsive in its inherent evil, its latent power to destroy.[1]

This awareness of the peculiarly technological aspects of the media has been attached most trenchantly to broadcasting, though fascination with technical novelty is an important feature of the early history of the cinema. Possibly the roots lay deeper, however; in popular revolts against industrialisation, for example. New technologies have altered both work and leisure but the relationship between these two is at least as important as the effect of scientific innovation on either.

A second area of concern surrounds the potential power of the mass media to influence ideas and beliefs and to manipulate behaviour. The kernel model of mass communications — the few addressing the many with impunity and omnipotence — has led to a research emphasis on effects and the dangers of persuasive communication. Propaganda and advertising have been the central problem areas explored. Much wartime research was aimed at investigating the effectiveness of hostile propaganda and

2

perfecting better techniques for combating it. This research, particularly in the United States, has left a lasting impression on later work, while in this country folk-memories of Lord Haw-Haw and the air of 'a friend in need' acquired by the BBC in wartime between them moulded much later discussion of the effects and dangers of broadcasting.

Similarly, the growth of the advertising industry and its use of the media stimulated unease about potential changes in popular attitudes, the creation of false needs and materialism, the promotion of secularisation and the spread of feelings of relative deprivation among large sections of the population. Denys Thompson was an important early exponent of this view,[2] and has recently restated it with undiluted pungency:

Advertising ensures a conforming population of consumers through its control of Press and T.V. . . . Its ethics powerfully suffuse the whole system of communication. As the theology of the status quo it aims at controlling our lives and keeping us on the consumer treadmill.[3]

Many such sentiments have limited their attack to advertising itself, its ethics and rhetoric, rather than its impact on the media. As with the concern about propaganda the effect on research has been to deflect the spotlight away from the 'villains' under attack and on to the 'victims'.

A third, and broader, concern arises from a long tradition of cultural criticism associated with such writers as Matthew Arnold, T. S. Eliot and F. R. Leavis, whose fear has been that the diffusion of culture inevitably creates a levelling downwards, that increased leisure is being wasted in exposure to the trivia of mass entertainment, and that the preservation of all that is best in English culture is both ignored and threatened by the new media. The large body of research work aimed at discovering ways of countering those tendencies is testament to the influence such views have carried.[4]

A further set of troubled beliefs relates to the discovery of vulnerable groups felt to be particularly susceptible to the influence of the media. By virtue of high exposure because of lack of alternative leisure resources, or unusual defencelessness because of ignorance or immaturity, these groups are felt to need special protection. Children and the working classes have both intermittently fitted these roles.

The concern for children is graphically illustrated by the title of one influential piece of American research, Frederick Wertham's *Seduction of the Innocent*[5]. Nor are these concerns particularly new. John Tobias writing about juvenile crime in the nineteenth century says that:

> The impact on the popular imagination made by Jack Sheppard, Dick Turpin and other heroes of crime was such that they had become almost legendary by the nineteenth century ... Contemporaries found that their names and adventures were familiar to many youngsters who did not know the name of the Queen of England.

The governor of one gaol was in no doubt of the root cause of his young inmates' delinquency, ' "It was them there penny numbers what I used to take in, sir." '[6]

Attention has turned not just to the impact of mass media on children's activities — their criminal behaviour, schoolwork, the monopoly of their leisure time acquired by the media — but on their beliefs, and attitudes to sex, religion and morality generally. The National Viewers' and Listeners' Association, a voluntary organisation formed in the mid 1960s around the critical views of its energetic secretary, Mary Whitehouse, has always made the allegedly damaging impact of broadcasting on children a major target in its campaigns. Mrs Whitehouse has often retailed how it was her discovery of the effect of television on the sexual behaviour of teenagers that led to the formation of the VALA.[7]

A similar regard for the innocence and vulnerability of less educated and sophisticated users of the media runs through both media practice and later research. Lord Reith, the first Director-General of the BBC, has become an archetype of the exponent of the media as tools for popular education and moral uplift, not least in the field of the arts. 'For years', Reith wrote in 1924, 'the man in the street has been content to be pleased with music which is easily and quickly assimilated, and therefore not always of the best.'[8] The task of the BBC was to wean him on to more exacting and worthwhile fare. Arguments about the role of censorship have often stressed the inverse relationship between cultural sophistication and vulnerability to mass communications, in attempts to justify censorship by price, or to stress the need for the most careful control to be applied to the most widely diffused material.

Judith Agassi, in an article discussing varying versions of the debate about 'the worker and the media', has described how cultural critics have tended to 'single out the working class as the special victim', and remarks on the way this view shaped, and was shaped by, research on propaganda.[9] Loss of religious faith, fecklessness, culturelessness and amorality are frequently held to be the result of exposing the working class to mass communications. As with children the concern has a long pedigree. An outraged Wordsworth, writing in 1800, was moved to remark that

a multitude of causes known to former times are now acting with a combined force to blunt the discriminating powers of the mind, and unfitting it for all voluntary exertion to reduce it to a state of almost savage torpor. The most effective of these causes are the great national events which are daily taking place, and the increasing accumulation of men in cities, where the uniformity of their occupations produces a craving for extraordinary incident which the rapid communication of intelligence hourly gratifies.[10]

5

There remains a final convergence of concern on the points at which the media interact with the state. This is defined as the effect of the mass media on the political system, both as actors within it and as carriers of the information required in political activities. Participation can be both indirect and subtle, or as direct as one famous editor of *The Times*, John Delane, who 'established such a position of ascendancy and commanded so many and so varied confidential contracts with Ministers who were anxious to secure his goodwill, that there was practically no state secret of which he was not informed within a few hours of its disclosure to the cabinet'.[11]

As well as influencing politicians the media can be used by them. Thus attention is turned on manipulation of the media by power holders, and in a more formal sense the control and limitation of the media by governments. To the extent that mass communications form public opinion, their relationship to the state is both an index of and a contributor to the effective power or lack of it exerted by popular demands. This is an area explored at greater length in chapter four.

A whole series of concerns and anxieties, then, have shaped awareness of the mass media and research on them. These have formulated the questions social science has been able to ask about the media and played a major part in limiting our knowledge about their operations.

THE RISE OF RESEARCH

Commercial interest in leisure activities long anticipated any serious social science concern in the area, and continues vastly to outweigh it in quantity. This meant that all information gathered was about uses of the media and their effects, rather than about the media themselves.

In Britain very little research of any kind is available before the 1930s. Thriving circulations in the newspaper industry and a fairly equitable distribution of advertising revenue after the First World War dampened enthusiasm for readership research. As the first shots in the 'circulation wars' of the 1930s were fired, however, circulation research came into demand. The Audit Bureau of Circulation opened in 1931, and in 1932 the first breakdowns of circulation figures were produced. From 1934 onwards the London Press Exchange surveys were a regular feature of research, and Odhams began their postal surveys and 'the John Bull census'.

The consumption orientation of this research was distasteful to the patrician controllers of the early development of broadcasting. Reith himself was against listener research, though his reluctance was rarely so clearly expressed as that of a senior member of his programme board in 1930, who felt that since

> the ordinary listener does not know what he likes, and is tolerably well satisfied, as shown by correspondence and licence figures, with the mixed fare now offered, I cannot escape feeling that any money, time or trouble spent upon elaborate enquiries into his tastes and preferences would be wasted.[12]

Since the war the massive growth of market research into a multi-million pound industry has enormously advanced the quantitative study of media consumption, though surprisingly little has been done in some areas, notably the cinema. However, little research has been informed by social science theory and its demands for quick thumbnail sketches of audiences have not required such an approach. Nor has there been, not surprisingly, much concern with production or the producers of media output.

Social science entered the field via the series of concerns sketched earlier. The first major social science project on the British media looked at 'Television and the child', at a time when newly aroused anxieties about the novel dangers of television were at a height.[13] The subsequent development of academic research continued in this vein, both addressing questions raised by public concern, but more restrictively, examining them in the terms set by this concern.[14]

Each approach has generated its own research methods and techniques. While commercial research frequently relies on quota sample surveys or discussion groups, psychologists concentrate on 'clinical' or experimental settings. Researchers on the literary side have mainly used qualitative content analysis, while sociologists have used more quantitative content analysis, participant observation, and stratified sample surveys. This mixture of techniques has produced a patchwork of structured information not always comparable, reconcilable, or even complementary. Many gaps remain, perhaps most of all in the study of the mass media organisations and the production of mass communications.

THE MEDIA AND THE AUDIENCE

This book is predominantly concerned with the mass media, as an industry and as social organisations, rather than with the effects of their products on their audiences. Inasmuch as the sociology of the mass media has an intrinsic coherence, it is in the study of the structural relationships within and between these organisations. The more diffuse area of mass communications is well·described and analysed elsewhere.[15] However, a brief review of the relationships between the media and their audiences will serve to introduce later discussions.

Audiences and the mass media interact on the basis of supply and demand. If we look at supply, interest concentrates on the rise of an industry and its changing economic context. If we look at demand the switch is to the mixture of processes which shape the cultures of different social groups which in turn produce different patterns of use, and of the requirements and needs brought to the media.

The term *mass* media and *mass* communication should not obscure the variations within the audience and the vastly different ways in which people use the media. Even television, the mass medium *par excellence,* has by no means a homogeneous reception. Young people in their teens watch far less television than older groups, though they make greater use of the radio. While working-class adults spend over nineteen hours a week in front of their set, the upper middle classes, with a greater range of leisure options available to them, devote less than fourteen hours to television. Nor will they be watching the same programmes at the same times. Even regional variations are important. In an average week anything up to ten different programmes may top the ratings in different viewing areas. And of course women, as every advertiser knows, watch more than men.[16]

Such variations are even more striking for the other media. Newspaper partiality is persistently a class-based phenomenon in Britain.[17] *The Times,* for example, is still the 'top people's' paper, with 78 per cent of its readership among the middle class, especially the professional middle class, and only 8 per cent from the unskilled working class. A popular tabloid like the *Daily Mirror,* on the other hand, can expect only about a quarter of its readers to be middle-class.[18] The attempts by newspapers to establish a large loyal readership with a large proportion among the younger, more affluent groups sought by advertisers, explain many of the recurrent stylistic changes seen in national newspapers.

Cinema-going also is by no means uniform throughout the population. The Screen Advertising Association classify 54 per cent of the population as 'cinema-goers', but in the fifteen to twenty-four age group this rises to 89 per cent, while among the over forty-fives only about a third make a habit of going to the cinema. The ratio of cinema admissions to population is over twice as high in Scotland, Wales, and the South-West as it is in London and the South-East.[19]

Books are at best a contender for the label mass media.

9

While both buying and borrowing have increased enormously in the last twenty years both remain of sectional importance. A report in 1965 estimated that 32 per cent of the population seldom or never used a library.[20] Probably less than 2 per cent of the population read 50 per cent of the books published.[21] While in greater London there is a bookshop for every 15,000 people, 49,000 share the same source in Staffordshire. Not surprisingly book ownership, reading, and buying are all strongly related to education, age and class.[22]

Striking though this patchwork of reception is, it still does not completely reveal the great variety of audiences of which the 'mass audience' is in fact composed. For many groups none of these media are primary. For example, for a great many adolescents the pop media, the magazines, records, and leisure facilities produced for the youth market, soak up the majority of the time and money they devote to the media.

This variegated picture has prompted one school of research to turn away from seeking the 'effects' of the media, to look instead for what 'uses and gratifications' audiences derive from them. That is, they investigated 'not what the media do to people but what people do with the media'. Researchers at Leeds University have isolated four categories of what they call 'media-person interactions'. These they call diversion (escape and emotional release), personal relationships (companionship and social utility), personal identity (reflecting on one's own life using media-derived material), and surveillance (of information and opinions in the wider world).[23]

This approach has successfully transcended simplistic notions of the 'escapist' uses attributed to audiences by many commentators. It is, however, as yet, limited by many empirical problems. The research is based on a limited range of programmes and respondents, and has not fully explored variability over time and social context. There are also more fundamental problems. Firstly the assumption that people actively *use* the media is problematic, as is the likelihood that specific programmes provide for specific gratifications. Secondly the gratifications in fact derived from a programme may be other than those a respondent can readily identify. Many entertainment programmes, for example, may inform or 'orientate', though it is unlikely that a viewer would recognise or admit this to be their prime function. Thirdly, for a sociologist the existence of a random series of pre-existent gratifications is less interesting than their distribution through the social structure, if indeed they exist in quite this way. So the question changes from one of which needs are satisfied by what sorts of programmes to one of which groups of people bring what sorts of demands to the media.[24]

The media do, nonetheless, have different meanings for different people, often independently of their overall consumption. A study of adolescents on probation in four areas of the East Midlands found that their involvement with television did not increase with their exposure to it.[25] When compared with control groups the amount of their viewing was not very different, but the probation sample were more attuned to 'exciting' material and to hero figures.[26] The relationship between exposure to media output and its salience is rarely direct or uniform.

The variety of social contexts within which media output is used suggests the problems attending any attempt to study mass communications as an isolated phenomenon. More than any other sociological topic mass communications overlaps most of the central interests of social science. To study mass communications without reference to a wide variety of other institutions and cultural processes would be like studying industrialisation as a problem in engineering technology. For several reasons the media do, however, deserve urgent sociological attention.

First, the massive growth of the mass media has increased their relevance and importance. In 1950 there were just over a third of a million television licences, by 1970 the figure was nearly 16 million. In the same period the number of book titles published each year nearly doubled, from 17,000 to over 33,000.

Secondly, the time spent by the British population in consumption of media produced articles has grown at a greater rate than leisure time. Television viewing averages over sixteen hours a week, radio listening over eight; together they far outrank all other leisure activities. Thirdly, the media have become totally dominant as a source of information for most people. In a recent survey 90 per cent of people asked about where they got information about what is going on in this country and in the world named television, the newspapers or radio.[27] This is hardly surprising but does place the media at the forefront of sociological concern. The rise of an increasing variety of pressure groups is a fourth reason for extending this interest. Many of the claims made by such groups are as emotive as they are influential, but serious research is seldom available either to challenge or to support their views.

Finally, the expanding economics of media production and consumption are an additional index of their importance. Advertising comprises roughly 1·5 per cent of the gross national product; advertising expenditure on television alone may run up to £20 million in some months, and totals over £700 million a year on all media. Personal expenditure on media products amounted to over £1,000 million in 1972 and, perhaps as a result, many media companies feature prominently among the largest industrial organisations in Britain.

These facts suggest the need for the media sociologist to look at the economics and history of the media in any survey of their organisation and effects. Chapter 2 looks at the history of the media and the way their present structure has emerged. Chapter 3 examines this structure in more detail and the economic context in which it operates. In Chapter 4 the internal social organisation of the media and the creative processes within them are discussed, before looking, in Chapter 5, at the relationship between the media and other key institutions. The final chapter discusses changes in the media as these are being affected by, and are themselves affecting, broader social changes.

The history and development of the media in Britain 2

For a large proportion of Britons television, the most completely diffused mass medium, is an innovation they have witnessed in their own lifetime. The other media have historical roots spreading back to the introduction of printing in the fifteenth century, to the vast impact on cultural change of industrialisation, and to the many subsequent technological and economic changes of the nineteenth and twentieth centuries.

In examining the sequential spread of the media in the United States Melvin DeFleur has suggested that each medium is adopted slowly at first, then very rapidly, finally flattening off as saturation point is reached or as a new medium takes over. In other words an S-shaped curve would describe the adoption of each technological innovation.[1] This approach sees the media as special instances of the more general phenomena associated with the diffusion of technical innovations. However, the particular circumstances of British history and geography prevent any transfer of these generalisations. This chapter describes some of these circumstances and their effects.

The growth of mass communications is a dual process. On the one hand it describes the development of an industry, on the other, the evolution of an audience. The relationship between the two is one of supply and demand for two basic social commodities; leisure facilities and information. Before describing in detail the history of each medium a general scheme describing this relationship will be outlined in the next page or two.

The demand for information and leisure facilities is determined by the time available for them, the affluence of the population seeking them and a variety of cultural factors reflecting social and geographical differences in the way such facilities are used. While legal and technical changes have facilitated a decline in working hours the overall increase in leisure time is a lot less than is frequently supposed. In many industries the need for overtime to supplement low wages lifts actual working hours well above the notional working week. The average number of hours worked in industry has declined very little in the last twenty years (from 47·8 hours in 1951 to 44·7 hours in 1971)[2] while the growth of conurbations has extended travelling times between home and work. Nevertheless, longer holidays and the growing proportion of retired people in the population mean that for many, more leisure can increase the demands they bring to the media. Many studies have described how the quality of this leisure varies for different occupational groups. For many white-collar workers leisure provides an opportunity for active participation in sport or in voluntary associations. For those in more gruelling employment leisure may be merely a period of recuperation between work periods. The relationship between work and leisure is a complex one, but in general it is clear that work experience is a central determinant of the amount and type of leisure demands an individual will make.

The affluence of a population is in effect its ability to exert demands. While the time available for media products may have increased, the range and extent of options available to different sections of the population will depend on their income, and more particularly on the amount of discretionary spending they can command. While the population as a whole spends roughly £1,000 million a year on the major media (television, cinema, Press, books and magazines), some groups contribute disproportionately to this total. Clearly the average annual figure of £60—£70 per

15

household is beyond the reach of many lower income groups, and heavily exceeded by many in the higher echelons. Table 1 shows the range of expenditure on some media products.[3] On average these categories of expenditure form about 4 per cent of the household budget. This is higher for low income groups, largely because expenditure on broadcasting licences is relatively inelastic (apart from the increasingly common extravagance of colour television). Actual expenditure on publications, broadcasting 'hardware', and visits to the cinema increases very sharply with income; for many, books and the cinema remain luxuries for which demand is highly elastic.

TABLE 1.

Household expenditure on media by selected income groups

Media	Average weekly expenditure (£) in the following income groups (£ per week)			As % total expenditure (all income groups)
	£15–20	£35–40	£80+	
Radios, televisions, musical instruments	£0.15	£0.34	£0.90	1·1
Books, newspapers, magazines, etc.	£0.39	£0.55	£1.15	1·6
Cinema admissions	£0.01	£0.05	£0.17	0·2
Radio/TV licences and rental	£0.37	£0.45	£0.68	1·3
Media expenditure as % total household expenditure	£4.91 (of £18.75)	£4.21 (of £32.99)	£3.98 (of £72.85)	4·2

Source. Adapted from *Family Expenditure Survey 1972.*

As well as the effect of leisure and affluence, demand for media facilities is shaped by a series of cultural factors which determine the ability people have to use these facilities and their attitudes to them. For the print media literacy is obviously crucial. While Britain is assumed to have near-universal literacy, reading for pleasure is by no means so ubiquitous. Life styles supporting the use of books and library membership, or allowing the facilities for quiet isolation are clearly differentially distributed through the class structure; such differences are often used to explain some of the problems of working-class children in coping with the demands of their schools.

Such life style differences also shape the ways audiences use the media, so that different groups make varying demands on what is superficially the same media output. It has generally been assumed, for example, that earlier maturity, growing adolescent affluence, and the emergence of a leisure industry catering for this new youth market have created a homogeneous 'youth culture', distinguishing the postwar generation in Britain by its life style and by its leisure activities. Recent research by Murdock and Phelps shows this to be too simple an analysis.[4] Discrete styles within 'pop' are adhered to by working-class and middle-class adolescents in different ways, and have totally distinct meanings and functions for them. The intellectualisation of 'progressive' pop finds its support among middle-class enthusiasts but is often rejected by working-class pop fans for whom the pop media are only one element in a diversified leisure culture. Young people still at school use the pop media as a complement to the rather different values of school culture. Middle-class girls with a high commitment to school and little or no access to either working-class 'street culture' or the wider range of activities open to adolescent boys have the greatest involvement in media 'pop culture'.

The supply side of the equation determines to a large extent how these diverse demands are met. The availability of

17

different media varies both geographically (in 1971 there were 47 cinemas in East Anglia but 232 in the Greater London Council area) and temporally (national radio, television and local radio have each taken some years to become ubiquitously available — it is an often noted irony that the country-dweller, who arguably has the greatest need for broadcasting, has usually been the last to receive it).

For most media, too, the supply is differentiated into a variety of competing or complementary sources. The print media, particularly books, are the most differentiated with well over 30,000 book titles published each year in recent years. The number of newspapers on the other hand has declined, and most readers of provincial newspapers no longer have any choice among competing voices.

Broadcasting had a single source in Britain until 1954. The compact geography of the country and Lord Reith's insistence on 'the brute force of monopoly' to underpin broadcasting's other goals maintained this situation until the advent of commercial television, and later local radio.

Technological changes further complicate the pattern of media supply, based often in underlying industrial and economic developments. Necessity, in the form of wars, imperial expansion, and commerce, has mothered a large proportion of the inventions which punctuate the history of the mass media. The steam printing press, wireless telegraphy, the cathode ray tube, satellites have all in turn recast the supply of media material and thus the range of options within which audiences exert their demands.

So we have two sets of factors in constant interaction. Demand, shaped by affluence, leisure time, and cultural variation, is exerted on a supply dependent on geographical and temporal availability, on differentiation and on technical changes. In looking at the history of the media we must concentrate, though not exclusively, on the supply, and here all the media follow a general historical pattern which falls· into two periods. In the first period production and distribution become separate social processes, and consumption becomes large-scale and impersonal. This is the process of industrialisation. In the second stage distribution and production come back together and tensions develop between consumption and production. This period is one of concentration and will be described in Chapter 3. The rest of this chapter describes how these processes have developed in each of the British media.

BOOKS AND PUBLISHING

The first important public for the printed word was the specialised professional public of church education. Lecture notes from ecclesiastical teachers were an inefficient form of mass reproduction, and education soon capitalised on the introduction to Britain of printing by Caxton in 1476. Before Caxton foreign printers had supplied the moral handbooks, French grammars and classics sought by the medieval nobility. The growth of the grammar schools preparing their charges for the professions provided a new market for native printers. Steinberg estimates that two-fifths of the books published by Caxton's successor were aimed at grammar school boys.[5]

Mercantilism in the Tudor and Stuart periods induced a steady growth in literacy and the number of printers gradually increased, though only under strict control by licence in Oxford, Cambridge, London, and later in York. After the Licensing Act of 1695 ended the Stationers' Company monopoly, however, printers began to appear in growing profusion; in London alone the number grew from twenty in 1662 to 103 in 1724.

As individual and court patronage of writers declined, to be replaced for half a century by party-based patronage, writers like Defoe were prepared to proclaim with equal eloquence the virtues of Whig or Tory according to their immediate employment. The Copyright Act of 1709 gave the author far greater control over his output, and though its effects did not begin to bite until later in the century it was crucial in the increasing separation of author and publisher which was the first stage in the eighteenth-century differentiation of the book trade. The second stage was the emergence of the booksellers, who as Ian Watt writes, 'occupied a strategic position between author and printer, and between both of these and the public'.[6] This was the age of Grub Street, representing what Goldsmith was to call 'that fatal revolution whereby writing is converted to a mechanic trade'. Speed, copiousness, and thus pulp prose were the order of the day. It heralded, too, the further decline of personal patronage and dedication, already on the wane as the more ingenious seventeenth century writers had exploited collective patronage and subscriptions.

Yet for all the increased reading of chap-books, ballads, broad-sheets, and religious works (*Pilgrim's Progress* had gone through 160 editions by 1792), the eighteenth century did not produce any substantial growth in literacy. Industrial work and child labour blunted the opportunities and demand for reading material of any kind and for education, though they did produce a new audience of leisured women and domestic servants for the developing novel. Laurence Stone estimates that the proportion of male literates in England only increased from 45 per cent in 1675 to 56 per cent in 1775.[7]

The biblical zeal of the Puritans was replaced by the cautious utilitarian teaching of industrialisation, while growing fear of radical excesses dampened the rate of educational diffusion. As Mandeville wrote ironically in 1723, 'Reading, writing and arithmetic . . . are very pernicious to the Poor . . . Men who are to remain and end their days in a laborious, tiresome, and painful station of life, the sooner they are put upon it at first the more patiently they'll submit to it for ever after.'[8] The major group of lower class readers were the Wesleyans, but 'the association of serious reading with what the non-Methodist world took to be sheer fanaticism may well have slowed the general spread of interest in books'.[9]

Late eighteenth-century radicalism and the instrumental education of industrialisation promoted reading and literacy after 1780; by 1790 Paine's *Rights of Man* had sold 200,000 copies. Industrialisation also provoked an upsurge in production of manuals of instruction of one kind and another. The *Athenaeum* complained in 1833 that, 'this is the age of the subdivision of labour, four men make a pin and two men describe it in a book for the working classes'.[10]

The wartime paper shortages forced paper prices up, and despite the popularity of Scott, novels were outsold by pamphlets and broadsheets describing trials, murders and a wide variety of salacious entertainment, often to massive audiences.[11] The description of Thurtell's trial in 1823 sold 500,000 copies, and the high (because taxed) cost of newspapers kept these circulations brisk until the 1870s, after which part-work novels were replaced by cheap one-volume reprints and magazine serialisations.

While prices were high publishers found themselves in the grip of the circulating libraries, whose power reached a peak in the 1870s. Thereafter their hold began to loosen as cheap 'railway novels', a growing middle-class public, and technical innovations in printing began to take effect. In 1800 paper production was just 11,000 tons per year, all of it handmade, but by 1860 production was 100,000 tons and nearly all of it mechanised. König's printing press, Stanhope's stereotyping, steam power and machine binding turned book production into a large-scale manufacturing industry, and the turn of the century saw the triumph of the penny book, symbolised by the opening of Dent's Everyman Library in 1906. The Net Book Agreement of 1899, by refusing discounts and preventing underselling had effectively killed the already waning circulating libraries.

The public library movement had been slow to expand,

despite the long-established voluntary libraries, especially those of religious bodies. A deaf recluse called Edward Edwards had campaigned vigorously in the 1840s for public libraries, to the point where their establishment became a feature of the reform movement. Enabling legislation in 1850 was a weak stimulus to rate supported libraries; only 334 had opened by 1896. They were opposed on the grounds that they brought literary trash to office boys, and by the drink lobby who feared they would keep people out of the pubs. The real growth in public libraries is a twentieth-century phenomenon, and it is only one of the influences that have transformed the book trade. But its significance can be seen in a glance at the number of books issued from lending libraries, increasing from 8 million annually in the 1870s to over 50 million in 1910, then, after the 1919 Public Libraries Act, to 85 million in 1923–24, soaring to 250 million in the late 1930s.[1 2]

The majority of books read today are borrowed from libraries or from other people. A survey in 1965 found that 37 per cent of the books people were reading were borrowed from libraries, and a further 32 per cent from other sources. Only 24 per cent had been bought.[1 3] Bookbuyers tend to be young, middle-class, and reasonably well-to-do. More men than women, and more older people, use public libraries.[1 4]

These factors represent a series of pressures on and changes within the book industry. Rising costs, especially of paper, have rapidly forced prices up; the price of hardback books doubled between 1963 and 1970. Library borrowing has grown rapidly since the war, from 312 million books issued in 1948–49 to over 600 million now. Yet library budgets have not kept up with rising costs, and only account for 15 to 20 per cent of book sales.[1 5]

At the same time the proportion of hardback sales has dropped in the face of what has come to be labelled 'the paperback revolution'. In 1960 there were under 6,000 paperback titles in print, in 1970 the figure was over 37,000.

Paperback and other rights (films, book clubs and so on) have become the cornerstone of publishing. Yet paperback publishing, and the other major growth area, educational publishing, require large-scale finance. Publishing has therefore increasingly become part of the multimedia industry so antipathetic to its traditional small-scale, personal, professional ambience. Publishers in groups, like Longman, Granada, Macmillan, and Thomson have all outgrown this stage of publishing and diversified into large-scale industries. In the search for bestsellers there has been an enormous increase in the number of titles (17,000 in 1950, 35,000 in 1973) though the annual production of new novels has remained constant at roughly 4,000 since 1950, a fact often taken to indicate 'the crisis of the novel'.

A further response is the internationalisation of publishing. Overseas markets, particularly in the 'Third World', have been quickly exploited by the larger publishers. By 1950 30 per cent of book production was exported, a figure which rose to 47 per cent by 1969. At the same time some British publishers have become partly or wholly American owned, though often only temporarily and not always successfully.[16] All these changes, as we shall see, are reflections of those in the other media.

THE PRESS

The development of British newspapers closely parallels that of book publishing; indeed publisher-printers were normally responsible for both until the eighteenth century. It is a story often told in terms of the romantic deeds of individual journalists and owners,[17] but the overall process is well summarised by a major figure of twentieth-century journalism:

The form which the British Press has taken, of popular

national papers dominating the market, was created largely by circumstances over which newspaper owners had little or no control; by the shape of the country and its railway system; by the existence of huge concentrated populations in a handful of linked towns; by the dominance of London over the provinces; and by the advanced structure of British business, which sought a national market for branded goods and needed a national Press for its sales campaigns.[18]

Wealthy patrons in the sixteenth century retained personal newswriters to bring them information of the Spanish Wars and the growth of foreign trade. The extension of this practice into a commercial Press through the seventeenth century saw the establishment of printed papers in London, and after the introduction of a weekly public post in 1673 of handwritten digests for the provinces.[19] Nonetheless the earliest important paper was the official *Gazette* started in 1665, and it was not until the close control of printing by the Chief Licenser ended in 1695 that the commercial Press really began to expand; a development signalled by the inauguration of the first daily newspaper, *The Courant,* in 1702.

The following years were dominated by the weekly magazines and the Grub Street journalists and pamphleteers[20] (two groups not always maintaining their distance from one another). Steele, Addison, and Defoe in their different ways shaped journalism for decades to come in serving the varying needs of the rising commercial class and the public of the coffee-houses. After 1750 the publisher-printers gave way to joint stock companies, giving the Press a secure economic base from which to fight battles for the extension of their activities, especially into politics. The right to report parliament (made illegal in 1729) became a symbol of this extension, and Dr Johnson's famous ability to recreate debates from minimal clues, and even to insert a fictional eloquence which was too good to be disowned by its putative authors, like the legendary abilities of 'Memory' Woodfall, were dramatic episodes in the process.[21] But the growth in power of the newspaper-reading class underlined by the conflict between the financial power of the City and the Commons was the real drive behind the rise of the Press to a position Macaulay was later to characterise as the Fourth Estate of the Realm.[22]

A second and even more trenchant battle was to follow between the emerging radical Press in the late eighteenth century and the subsequent 'taxes on knowledge' aimed at curbing their influence. Cobbett, Wooller, Carlisle, Hetherington and others defied the various duties imposed on paper to produce the 'unstamped Press' often achieving enormous circulations against fierce opposition; between 1831 and 1835 there were 800 arrests on charges under the various acts of repressive legislation. Yet when stamp duty was massively reduced (from fourpence to one penny) in 1836, the major beneficiaries were the middle-class papers.

The Times, with a circulation of two or three thousand in the 1820s, jumped from 11,000 in 1837 to 60,000 in 1855. More than any other paper it had captured the voice of respectable reform (opposing the government on Peterloo, for example). The issues of reform and war enormously stimulated the demand for all newspapers, and the sale of paper stamps (one useful index of print runs) rose from 16 million in 1800 to 30 million in 1830, while the population had grown only from 10·5 to 16 million,[23] despite prices which still largely excluded even the lower middle class. Readership remained much greater than circulation figures suggest.

Most of all, this was the great growth period of the Sunday Press. Inheritors of the demotic broadsheet tradition, comparatively cheap because untaxed (many were untouched by the 1819 Stamp Act because they carried so little news), widely bought by coffee-houses, clubs, pubs, and barbers' shops, their circulation rapidly outstripped the dailies, and has remained ahead ever since. By 1850 the total Sunday circulation was well over a quarter of a million, more than four times that of the dailies; *Lloyd's Weekly,* the *Illustrated London News,* and the *News of the World,* were each selling 50,000 and more even before the Stamp Tax was removed in 1855.

As prices dropped after the ending of the Stamp Tax (Advertising Tax had ended in 1853), developing literacy and the expanding middle-class public began to push circulations up rapidly, exploiting the possibilities of steam-printing and cheaper paper to the full. Individual purchases replaced collective subscriptions and daily provincial newspapers proliferated.

This rapid expansion was graphically represented by the rise of the *Daily Telegraph.* Starting on the day Stamp Tax ended in 1855, it dominated the next thirty years. The 'paper of the man on the knifeboard of the omnibus', it appealed directly to the ambitious optimism of the new ascendant Victorian lower middle class, reporting fully on imperial expansion, the Boer wars, European developments and other less serious audience-attracting features.

Changing styles in the second half of the nineteenth century revolutionised the British Press still further as it became part of that embryonic entertainment industry which included professional sport and the music halls. Typographical and photographic techniques imported from America, the use of headlines and interviews, the brisk, factual 'reporting' of the news agencies,[24] sports news, all those elements in fact which Matthew Arnold characterised as 'the new journalism', transformed the appearance of national dailies and helped boost their already rising circulations.

The Sunday Press still maintained its lead, much stimulated by the Jack the Ripper murders and similar traditional fare. As Raymond Williams remarks, 'no lion of the new journalism would have had anything to teach eighteenth-century journalists in the matter of crudeness and vulgarity'.[25] By 1896 *Lloyd's Weekly News* had passed the million mark. New bright weeklies like *Tit-Bits* exploited the new styles and public so prosperously that Alfred Harmsworth, whose *Answers* was one of the most successful of the weekly penny papers, was prompted to remark that 'we have struck a goldmine'.

Harmsworth, later Lord Northcliffe, was quicker than most to see the relevance of the 'retail revolution' for the Press. The depression of 1873—94 had led to bigger companies, and competitive brand name advertising. Mass consumption entailed mass selling, and the buoyant daily press was the ideal advertising medium. The alliance of this development to American journalistic techniques, the possibilities of the new linotype process, and the recognition of an expanding public are normally designated 'the Northcliffe Revolution', though far better seen as one important stage in the continuing industrialisation of the Press. Harmsworth, 'the innocent genius of newspapers',[26] began the *Daily Mail* in 1896, and the *Daily Mirror* in 1903, the latter the first daily to sell a million. Both papers, and the *Daily Express*, the first paper to carry news on the front page, derived much of their income from the display advertising of department stores.

This major change in the economic base of the Press was the beginning of a period of concentration, in which circulation grew, the number of papers declined, and ownership was delivered into fewer and fewer hands. The entry of financiers into the Press in the 1920s, including Inveresk, Rothmere, the Berry brothers and Lord Cowdray, quickly consolidated this trend. By 1929 these four controlled roughly half the daily circulation.

The ensuing battles for readers in the 'circulation wars' of the 1930s in effect created a mass popular daily Press for the first time. The national daily circulation doubled from 1920

27

to 1939, and between 1924 and 1935 there was a 72 per cent increase in the staff of these papers. With newsprint actually getting cheaper commercial competition could absorb lavish expenditure to the extraordinary position where, in 1934, 40 per cent of the staff of popular national dailies were doorstep canvassers.[27] The casualty of these conflicts was the diversity of titles. From 1921 to 1937 the number of national papers dropped from twelve to nine, the number of provincial dailies from forty-one to twenty-eight. But in trebling circulations in the period from 1900 to the Second World War, economic consolidation based on advertising revenue and industrial concentration had created the mass Press market.[28]

The circulation wars were abruptly interrupted by the wider conflicts of World War Two. The period since 1945 has been one of recurrent crisis for the British national Press, completing the process of concentration in response to a whole new series of pressures, particularly after the ending of newsprint rationing which for a time made advertising revenue relatively easy to attract. Since then labour and production costs have soared, forcing cover prices up very rapidly, especially in the 1960s. As a result fewer people buy two newspapers and many have stopped buying a daily newspaper at all. Between 1961 and 1971 sales of national dailies dropped by 11 per cent.

This trend, however, hides variations within the Press; in the same period sales of the serious or 'quality' papers rose by 21 per cent, while the popular Press lost 15 per cent of their circulation (and it is the populars which are most dependent on circulation revenue). Advertising growth has been concentrated in the classified field which is primarily found in the 'quality' Press. Very few national newspapers now make profits, and the deaths of major titles have littered the recent history of the Press.

The response has been twofold. Firstly newspapers have merged into groups, either with each other, with provincial chains, or with other publishing interests. In 1973 three

28

groups controlled between them 72 per cent of the national daily circulation and 86 per cent of the Sunday circulation. The second response has pushed newspapers into industrial groups engaged in a wide variety of activities both in the media and elsewhere. These changes again reflect, as in publishing, general trends within all the media industries.

CINEMA

The British cinema was not modified by the late Victorian entertainment industry but produced by it. The first paid moving picture show took place in London in 1896, the same year in which Marconi took out a British wireless patent and the *Daily Mail* first appeared. Growing out of the commercialisation of other entertainments the early films were controlled by music-hall proprietors and travelling fairground showmen. Of the two, it was the latter who had an enduring effect. 'While cinema was a passing fancy in the music-hall it is to the fairground showmen that the cinema owes its ultimate success.'[29]

The subsequent rise and fall of the cinema follows the pattern already outlined for the print media. Small-scale beginnings rapidly became absorbed in technological developments which required large-scale finance. At the same time production, distribution, and exhibition became differentiated as the market expanded. Finally the pressures of decline have forced the cinema industry to concentrate its resources and diversify its interests into more successful industrial enterprises.

The small shop-shows soon gave way to the 'picture palaces' after 1906, until there were four or five thousand theatres open by 1914. The boom in exhibition and the rising costs of cinema technology led to larger companies and the attraction of large-scale finance into the industry. Rachel Low calculates that between 1908 and 1910 capital in the industry rose from £110,000 to over £3 million, while the number of companies soared from three to nearly 300.[30] Film exhibition itself became an industry, based initially on the stockpiling of films by early showmen. As film producers competed for the favours of the exhibitors the open sale of films declined, to be replaced by a hiring system, bringing with it the middlemen or renters.

Although many cinemas closed during the First World War, and admission prices rose because of the wartime Amusement Tax (which remained until 1924), the interwar years saw the creation of a vast national cinema-going audience. As Briggs remarks, 'over a long period the cinema did not so much divert an older audience from other kinds of entertainment as create an enormous new one.'[31] The result was the further extension of prewar industrialisation as large-scale finance poured in and film exhibitors grew into chain circuits. High and rising rental prices favoured the bigger companies and the remnants of the open market were swept aside by the formation of the Kinematograph Renters Society in 1918. At a dinner of the Exhibitors' association in 1920 Lord Burnham was moved to observe that 'the high financiers of the world are flocking into the cinema industry'.[32] The statistics of the boom are astounding. Capital in the industry rose from £15 million in 1914 to £70 million in 1929. In 1917 ninety circuits controlled 429 cinemas; by 1930 167 circuits controlled about 1,000. Nearly 1,000 cinemas were built between 1924 and 1932.

Among the first to suffer the side effects were the provincial theatres. But at the same time as exhibition was expanding the world cinema industry was dominated by the growth of Hollywood, and British film-makers were losing their grip on both audiences and exhibitors. So drastic was the impact of American production that by 1926 the proportion of British films exhibited had fallen to one in twenty.[32] Legislation in 1927 attempted to counter this trend, but was frequently circumvented by the use of 'quota quickies' — short cheap films made merely to satisfy statutory demands — and later by American investment in British production.[33] (A similar Act in 1948 conceded the inevitable by limiting the quota to exhibition and ignoring renters and distributors.)

The circuits gradually coalesced and by 1944 a third of the cinema seats were owned by three chains. Gaumont-British and Odeon, the two smaller chains, were taken over by Rank in 1941, leading to a monopoly inquiry in 1944.[34] This new chain and ABC, which started as a production company in 1928, were to become the twin giants of postwar film exhibition.

Admissions continued to rise through the Second World War to a peak in the mid-1940s. The war itself was a mixed blessing for films, packing the cinemas but killing European production and establishing complete dominance by Hollywood. The history of the British cinema since then has been one of continual crisis. The drop in attendances since the war is dramatic; from 1,635 million in 1946 right down to 163 million in 1972. In the same time the number of cinemas has shrunk from 4,703 to 1,482.

The major cause is, of course, television, especially after the arrival of commercial television and the spurt in set ownership in the 1950s. Spraos has argued convincingly that the latter was the more lethal factor.[35] Montagu suggests that the cinema sold a habit, movie-going, which was replaced by an easier habit, television viewing.[36] Whatever the explanation the pressures on the cinema industry have been enormous, resulting in government assistance, concentration, contraction, and a reliance on American finance.

Government aid has taken several forms.[37] Legislation has ensured that a quota of British films are exhibited, though this has not protected British film production in the way intended since definitions of 'British films' have allowed American financed films into the quota. Secondly, a levy on seat prices, made statutory in 1957, provides funds which are redistributed among British-made films, proportionately to their box office success. Thirdly, the National Film Finance Corporation, formed in 1949, exists to provide funds for domestic film production, particularly through support of *British Lion*. However, the recent failure of the latter has prompted the NFFC to withdraw from independent support of films, and instead to concentrate on financing strictly commercial films in conjunction with a private consortium.[38]

Nonetheless the pressures remain. Exhibition of films has consolidated into two major chains, EMI and Rank, both giants in the media industries, who also control film studios, artists, distribution, and a variety of related activities. As Kelly noted in 1966 'power in the film industry in the long run lies in the hands of the cinema circuits'.[39]

A final response has been the entry of American money into British films. As the domestic market in the USA slumped in the wake of television, British and other European film industries received increasing American finance.[40] The proportion of British feature films on the two main circuits which were American financed doubled from 43 per cent in 1962 to a peak of 88 per cent in 1968. However, problems in the American film industry have depleted much of this support since then, and the proportion has fallen steadily.[41] For the film industry the twin processes of industrial differentiation and subsequent concentration have been sharper, and more dramatic than in any of the other media.

BROADCASTING

The last major media to develop, radio and television, exhibit a rather different organisational evolution from the previous examples; they arose after the Industrial Revolution and required the mass urban public and technological advances that industrialisation had induced. They have been unique, too, in that for a substantial period in broadcasting history the monopoly of production and distribution was held by a state-controlled body.

Experimental work in this country, mainly by Marconi at Chelmsford, made little impact before the First World War, and during the war amateur radio was banned by the General Post Office. Amateur wireless associations had already begun to flourish, carefully licensed by the Post Office, and grew rapidly after Marconi started irregular experimental transmissions in 1920. These quickly attracted attention both from the other media (the *Daily Mail* was alert in spotting the promotional possibilities in the novelty of wireless) and from the electrical industry. In 1922 six companies combined to form the British Broadcasting Company, and the Post Office agreed to license only those sets made by the new organisation. The Company appointed John Reith as General Manager in December 1922, and he spent the next four years demonstrating, as he was later to put it in his autobiography, that 'whatever was in the interests of broadcasting must eventually be in the interests of the wireless trade'.[42]

As successive official committees discussed the new medium it became clear that Reith was virtually alone in having a clear vision of the organisational form these interests should take. His conception of 'public service broadcasting', as Briggs has analysed it, had four crucial elements.[43] Firstly, broadcasting was to be unsullied by the profit motive, though this was a limitation confined to programme production rather than equipment manufacturing. Secondly, national coverage to serve the whole community was essential. Thirdly, unified control, in Reith's famous phrase 'the brute force of monopoly', was deemed essential for both technical and social reasons. Finally public service entailed the maintenance of high standards, a notion that became transmuted in the following years into the idiosyncratic combination of middle-class ethics, stern Christianity,

33

patrician culture and schoolmasterly morality that have become inextricably linked with the Reithian period of the BBC and its aftermath.

The formation of the British Broadcasting Corporation from the Company in 1927 thus drew on twin influences. 'Without the initiative of business enterprise there would have been no BBC, without a concept of public service there would have been no corporation'.[4 4] By March 1927 over 2·26 million licences had been issued, a figure which doubled by 1933. By 1939 virtually the whole population had access to one programme, and the BBC itself had a staff 5,000 strong.

In this period television was still in its technological infancy, though its scientific antecedents reach back to the discovery of the electrochemical effects of light by Becquerel in 1839. But it was not until the development of the thermionic valve and the multistage amplifier that television became a real possibility.[4 5] In this country Baird had publicly demonstrated television as early as 1925, but the device did not emerge from the laboratory until 1929 when the BBC cooperated in experimental transmissions with Baird. In 1932 the Corporation took over transmission itself. Real progress still awaited the further development of the vacuum cathode-ray tube, delaying regular full transmissions until 1936, but the station closed at the outbreak of war.

The postwar development of broadcasting consisted primarily of two changes; the replacement of radio by television as the major medium and the introduction and growth of an alternative, commercial network. The war itself transformed the BBC into an enormous organisation (with under 5,000 employees in 1938 and over 11,000 by 1945). Television was reintroduced after the war, but not until the introduction of commercial television did the sale of sets really accelerate, though high prices and the residual attractions of alternative leisure patterns were as important as the anticipation of independent television in delaying the process.

By 1953 there were still only just over two million television licences. The campaign for commercial television was waged against a backdrop of both popular and governmental indifference or even antipathy. However, wartime experience of Radio Luxembourg and Radio Normandie, as well as the American Forces Network, had converted many to a lighter style in broadcasting, and opposition to the BBC monopoly was not uncommon in the Conservative Party. Allied with advertising and equipment manufacturing interests, commercial enthusiasts produced 'perhaps the most remarkable exhibition of political lobbying this country has ever seen'.[46]

The commercial television channel eventually opened in 1954. Although the increase in viewing it stimulated was slow at first, the growth after 1956 was extremely rapid. Television licences climbed from 3 million in 1954 to 8 million in 1958, 13 million in 1965, and arrived at virtual saturation point at 15 million in 1968. Whereas just 10 per cent of homes had sets in 1950, by 1963 only 10 per cent were without. Since 1950 radio only licences have steadily dwindled in numbers, overtaken by combined licences by 1958 and finally conceding defeat by disappearing in 1971. Nonetheless it has probably been the cinema rather than radio that has suffered the greatest impact of television.[47]

Saturation has placed television in the same set of pressures as we have seen surrounding other media. When there is no increase in the broadcasting audience there can be no increase in advertising revenue, unless broadcasting time is expanded, as indeed occurred in 1972 after a resurgence in the advertising industry. In the 1960s advertising had grown comparatively slowly, and with depressed profits in some of those industries providing the bulk of television advertising, such as food, the notion that ownership of a commercial television company was a 'licence to print money' withered somewhat. Costs increased by 50 per cent in the late 1960s and programme origination declined.[48]

35

Among the effects has been the familiar one of concentration. Five of the fifteen ITV companies serve over three-fifths of the audience and receive two-thirds of the commercial network's income. Familiar also are the well-developed links with other media organisations, particularly the Press, increasing production for overseas markets, and involvement in wider industrial activities. The BBC too has had to respond to financial pressure and to the new pressures of competition for audiences. Some of the results are discussed in later chapters.

All the media, then, in varying ways, have gone through a dual process, firstly of industrialisation and secondly of concentration. The different forms of concentration and other organisational features are described in more detail in the next chapter.

The structure and organisation of   3
the media

The last chapter described the way the mass media have evolved into complex and diversified organisations. In the course of this growth the prominence of their public provision of information and leisure has attracted to the media the attention of legislators, moralists and others concerned to apply public supervision to the structure of mass communications. Broadcasting especially, because of its initial national importance and the technical limitations on diversity, has grown up under an umbrella of public control. Against this the process of industrialisation described in Chapter 2 has resulted in commercial media whose activities are licensed both by law, and by bodies of control set up by the media themselves to protect their own best interests.

The second aspect of formal organisation is fused from the compound of financial arrangements by which the media perpetuate their activities. Far from being a separate concern, the economics of the media are an intrinsic part of understanding the sociology of their organisation.[1] The second half of this chapter describes the problems of social organisation in the contemporary media as these relate to underlying problems of resources, ownership, and changing leisure patterns.

MEDIA AND PUBLIC REGULATION

There are three types of mass media organisation which relate public regulation to their operations. Firstly there are government controlled media, whose explicit function is to convey government information uncritically and comprehensively. In many countries the major mass media are organised in this way, particularly in poorer countries where governments are the only bodies capable of providing the financial backing for a national Press or broadcasting service. Government ownership in such a situation need not necessarily imply total control over contents though the temptations are great. In Britain no newspapers or broadcasting stations are controlled directly by government, though a historical vestige remains in the shape of the *London Gazette,* published since 1665 to provide official accounts of government activities. The *Gazette* continued as the most successful provider of foreign news for nearly a century, and is still the official government newspaper, though now best known as the source for Premium Bond winning numbers, as well as for official appointments and the like. The decline of the *Gazette* in the eighteenth century was prompted by the development of the commercial Press, and this pattern is the normal sequence unless government media themselves adopt a commercial base.

The external services of the BBC are under the direct control of the Corporation, though the extent of government involvement in these operations is sometimes uncertain and not devoid of controversy. The British external broadcasting services, although having an output smaller than that of the USSR, the USA, China or Germany, nevertheless broadcast over 700 hours a week in English and 39 other languages. Unlike normal BBC operations, they are supported directly by a government grant-in-aid, which in 1972 came to about £14 million, including a monitoring service also operated by the external services.[2]

Government controlled information diffusion comes directly from two other sources, the Central Office of Information and the Information Divisions of the various ministries. These channels differ from the conventional mass media only in their total concentration on information — any entertainment value in government reports is usually unintentional — and because their primary target audience is very often the media rather than the general public directly. Nonetheless much government information is available through retail outlets, and this system is not essentially different from that of the other mass media.[3] The Central Office of Information, like the HMSO, is a common service department, and deals with general advertising, exhibitions, films and publicity about government and public activities. With an advertising expenditure of £8 million in 1971—72 the COI is far and away the largest advertiser in the country (the top commercial advertiser, the Co-op, spent only a quarter of this figure). Government home information services are run by each of the ministries, publicising their work, providing material for journalists and for the general public. The specific audience aimed at varies from ministry to ministry, for example the Foreign Office is one of the most media-conscious, whereas social service and employment ministries provide information more directly to the public. The flow of information into the political system, especially the less formal aspects of, for example, the lobby system, are described in Chapter 5. But the scale of government communications, as well as their functions as primary sources for the mass media, make them essential for consideration in any broader view of mass communications.

The second sort of public mass media organisation is the semi-official statutory body. Based in a widespread seventeenth-century model, the licensing monopoly, the structure of the BBC is a unique survivor of this system, though the special features of the Corporation derive more from the limited understanding of broadcasting in the 1920s and the vision and determination of Lord Reith, than any conscious awareness of a historical model. Probably a more immediate and prosaic precedent was the Port of London Authority. The BBC as an 'organisation within the constitution', is not directly the responsibility of a minister. Its closeness to government, however, has always been a point of dispute, and never more so than when, in its first year as a Corporation, the BBC faced a series of decisions about its reporting of the General Strike. Lord Reith's frequently quoted maxim that 'since the BBC was a national institution and since the Government in this crisis were acting for the people . . . the BBC was for the Government', has often been discussed, and cited as evidence of the roots of broadcasting policy in a historical pro-government posture established by Reith. However, relationships between the political system and broadcasting are more complex than such an explicit philosophy implies. Formally the BBC, though not directly responsible to parliament, is under public control as a non profit making corporate body established by Royal Charter. The Corporation itself comprises a Chairman, Vice-Chairman and ten Governors, who are part-time, and work through a permanent executive staff. They are all appointed in effect by the government. The Minister for Posts and Telecommunications licenses the BBC to broadcast and determines the conditions under which it can do so.

The BBC, of course, actually produces the programme material for which it is responsible. The third type of public regulatory agency to be considered does not originate material, though it does oversee it. The Independent Television Authority, which in 1972 became the Independent Broadcasting Authority to include commercial radio under its aegis, does not make programmes, though it has a limited and unused statutory entitlement to produce experimental educational programmes. The Authority in fact merely selects and gives contracts to programme companies, who themselves make programmes in what has become a federal regional system. The IBA itself owns and operates transmission facilities for which the companies pay a rental fee, and is also responsible for the balance of output, and for the monitoring and ultimate control of advertising. The

Authority's structure as a corporate body is not unlike that of the BBC's governors, comprising a Chairman, Deputy-Chairman and nine members. Fifteen companies produce the programmes on a purely commercial basis, except for news which is produced by the jointly owned non-profit making Independent Television News. The problems of a body which does not produce programmes and which is attempting to assert public control over commercial organisations have been recurrent and occasionally critical.[4] On the one hand it is argued that the only acceptable and viable support for an alternative broadcasting organisation must come from advertising, and that the accountability to public service requirements is a civilised bonus. On the other hand is the view that in the attempt to reconcile the demands of the market and of independent control and standards the commercial power of the production companies is bound to prevail.

Akin to the Independent Broadcasting Authority are those bodies which, while concerned with regulation or licensing of media products, are based within the industry rather than imposed on it by legislation. The British Board of Film Censors (BBFC) and the Press Council are the prime examples of this type of relationship. Local authorities first concerned themselves with films because of the fire risks involved in public exhibition, and eventually gained some say in the matter by virtue of the Cinematograph Act of 1911. The safety aspects of the legislation were interpreted very widely by many authorities, to include times of exhibition and increasingly the subject matter of films. To meet this threat the film industry set up its own censorship board, the BBFC, which began work in 1913. Gradually the present system evolved whereby the BBFC issues certificates which are generally, but in no legal sense necessarily accepted by local authorities. It is a system with many built-in problems, though its flexibility is a major advantage. One primary object is protection of the industry, and to this end much of

41

the Board's work is in an advisory capacity during production, by giving guidance about what is likely to be passed or given a particular grade of certificate. The explicit link with the industry has gradually declined, however; the Board's income derives from fees charged to the large number of individual producers who submit films for viewing, and its finances are vetted by the Association of Kinematograph Manufacturers, which represents the makers of exhibition equipment and so on.

Local authorities have tended to be more liberal than the Board in passing films, and a new intermediate certificate category was introduced in 1970 with the intention of liberating the 'X' grade and allowing a wider flexibility at that end of the scale. In fact the number of films refused certificates has continued to increase, as indeed it has done ever since the war. Since 1946 the number of films submitted to the Board has declined by roughly 50 per cent, while the number rejected has increased steadily from nil to 29 in 1972.[5]

Unlike the BBFC the Press Council is not concerned with prior censorship but with *ex post facto* adjudication of newspaper practice. The Council was set up after widespread concern about proprietorial restrictions on free expression due to limited Press ownership, especially as such concerns were expressed in the Royal Commission on the Press of 1947—49. In fact the Council did not begin operations until 1953, and in its first few years had little impact on Press or public. Various anxieties about Press behaviour in the 1960s, engendered partly by a conservative reaction to diminishing journalistic and stylistic inhibitions, partly by a radical concern about the continuing decline in choice, and partly because of specific lapses during, for example, the Profumo affair and the Vassall spy case, led to criticism of the Council itself. In Francis Williams's view 'the Press Council was too much like a doting mother with a child accused of delinquency'.[6]

The 1962 Royal Commission on the Press subsequently recommended changes in the Council's constitution, so that it should have a lay chairman and lay membership, and that it should report on changes in ownership and control of the Press. These recommendations were implemented and the proportion of lay members was increased in 1972. The Council now comprises an independent Chairman, twelve representatives of various proprietorial associations, eight representatives of journalists' and editors' associations, and ten members of the public. The theory of the Council has been set out by its Chairman: 'The concept of the Press Council was based on the theory of self-discipline — a body speaking with the voice of the Press which can lay down standards of ethics . . . '[7] As well as this diffuse function the Council represents the industry to government and overseas, and receives and adjudicates on complaints about the Press. However, it only receives about 400 such complaints each year, chooses as appropriate for adjudication about a tenth of these, and upholds the grievance in about twenty cases.

Both these bodies have a general role of translating public concerns and changing moral climates into codes of practice. Neither has enormous power over media production, though the BBFC has considerably more than the Press Council. As buffers between the media and their publics they act as proxy lay critics and may attempt to emasculate or replace demands for public accountability or access. Their composition, the sanctions they can apply, their legal status and social impact would all bear closer examination than has yet been attempted.

MEDIA ECONOMICS

Most of the cultural products supplied by the media are market commodities; they have to be sold and they have to be sufficiently profitable to persuade the organisations that provide them that it is worth continuing to do so. Two exceptions to this mundane but crucial observation characterise the British media. First, the major broadcasting organisation, the BBC, makes no profit; indeed it accumulates a deficit, and is run as a public corporation. This does not mean it is not cost-conscious, and indeed its eagerness to compete for audiences has frequently attracted criticism. Secondly many national newspapers, probably the majority, are not profitable, though they all belong to industrial groups that are. There is a third group of unprofitable media on the fringe of normal commercial practice. This group includes the 'underground' Press and the marginal political Press. The often shortlived 'underground' papers, rooted in a 'countercultural' life style have circulated largely among the young urban middle class, and in the main have rarely been as significant as their American equivalents.[8] Some have become commercially successful and in turn commercial in operation. Fringe political newspapers, particularly when linked to a political organisation, are nearer in purpose and circulation to the nineteenth-century radical Press, and are also less likely to attract advertising revenue available to the countercultural papers from related leisure pursuits.

There are four main sources of revenue for culture-producing organisations. The first is directly from sales of the product. For book publishing this is the only source of finance, while at the other extreme sales provide no income to the producers of commercial television programmes (except for programmes sales within the network, which are not meant to produce profits, and exports which certainly do). In 1972, average weekly household expenditure on the media and entertainment was higher than that on clothing, or household durables. A total of £1,010 million was spent on books, newspapers, magazines, cinema tickets, and broadcasting licences and rentals, not including the sets themselves and the vast array of related leisure products, many of which derive from the same industrial complex.[9]

The second source of revenue comes from advertising. Here the opposite applies to the previous case, in that as a financial basis advertising is irrelevant to books but the lifeblood of commercial broadcasting. Advertising grew as an industry after the development of the competitive selling of branded goods on a large scale in the nineteenth century and, as described earlier it was the Press that first captured retailers' attention as a medium for advertising. The growth of the industry in the twentieth century has been rapid, from a total expenditure of £20 million in 1907 to nearly ten times that figure in 1956, and over £700 million in 1972. In recent years this rise has been largely accounted for by rises in space and production costs, and as a percentage of the gross national product advertising expenditure has in fact been slowly declining since 1960.[10] This should not disguise the central importance of advertising to the mass media.

One interesting change has been in the distribution of advertising revenue among the media. This is illustrated in Table 2. Revenue from advertising and sales distinguishes different types of newspaper even more clearly than tone and style. For the 'populars' advertising provides only about a third of their income, but comprises as much as three-quarters of the revenue of the quality or serious Press. An upsurge in available advertising can provide support for a new television channel or stimulate demand for an extra system of local radio stations. A downturn can change the character and diversity of, for example, the range of specialised, hobby and general interest magazines. It is in this long-term determination of viability that the significant 'influence' of advertising on the media is to be found, rather than in instances of the malign subversion of integrity. One obvious example is the size of newspapers, which is directly dependent on advertising revenue. In an extreme case the fact that a newspaper is not attractive to advertisers, because, for

45

TABLE 2

Distribution of advertising among media[1]

Media	1938	1948	% distribution 1954	1964	1972
National newspapers	25	14	17	21	18
Regional newspapers	27	31	31	24	27
Television	—	—	—	25	25
Cinema	3	4	3	1	1
Magazines and periodicals	15	13	19	11	9
Trade and technical journals	12	16	13	9	9
Other	18	22	17	9	11
Total expenditure (£ million)	59	79	157	416	708

example, its readership is too poor, may condemn it to extinction even with a large readership. This explanation is often advanced for the demise of the *News Chronicle* in 1960, although other obituary theories have been offered.

The third source of income for the media is from public subscription, normally through licence fees. Public broadcasting is the only medium which earns its livelihood in this way. The licence fee is in fact paid to the government, and passed on to the BBC after deducting a sum for the cost of collection. Radio licence fees started life at a cost of ten shillings in 1922; by the time radio only licences were abolished in 1971 the combined fee was £6, and has since risen again to £7 or £12 for a colour television. As is often indignantly pointed out by the BBC, this is among the lowest licence fees in Europe. The BBC does derive a little income from sales, publications and miscellaneous enterprises, but in 1971—72 all but about £1·75 million of its £115 million income derived from licence fees.

The fourth way media derive financial support for their operations is from the government. This can work in a variety of ways. Chapter 2 described the various aids received by the cinema industry. Television receives government assistance in three ways. Firstly the BBC receives the grant-in-aid for the external services described earlier. Secondly the BBC has to turn to the government to fill the gap between its expenditure and income. Colour television, with the additional licence income it induced, has been a boon to the BBC in supplying an alternative plug for this gap. By March 1971 the deficit had accumulated to over £6 million, but a year later had dropped to £2·5 million. The political potential of this 'subsidy' is sometimes described as though it were a sword of Damocles held over the BBC by governments, though no real evidence about the substance of this charge exists. The logic of the situation, as Stuart Hood has described it, is that 'the drive for maximisation of audiences has a political motive, which is that when the BBC applies for an increase in the licence fee it feels it must be in a position to show that it attracts a large proportion of the total audience'.[12] At a micropolitical level the deficit might act as a latent threat during any sniping war between BBC and government in short-term confrontations. The third support by government for television is the rather negative one of reduction in the levy on advertising revenue. This tax was introduced in 1965 and by 1969 represented nearly 40 per cent of costs for the major commercial television companies. However it was substantially reduced in 1971 and in 1973 was modified to apply to profits rather than revenue.

In a few countries, notably in France (through various tax concessions), Holland (through an enforced subsidy from broadcast advertising revenue) and Scandinavia, commercial newspapers receive considerable support from the public purse. Although Britain has no direct system for aid for newspapers government advertising is an important indirect route of official support. The scale of such advertising was indicated earlier, and its uneven distribution among newspapers has occasioned dissatisfaction in the past.[13]

Financial support for the media by government is one strand in a broader debate about the relationship of the media to society. One side of this debate argues that the cultural centrality of communications make it imperative that the media are under public control. Thus the Press and broadcasting might both be controlled by national foundations and financed or subsidised by taxation, with guaranteed pluralism the object of such a system. The other side of this coin is the view that the marketplace for ideas will ensure the success of such sources as contribute worthily to public information and delight, while condemning to morbidity only those media whose own deficiencies are too great to deserve an audience. These two views far from exhaust this particular debate, but do represent two of the major contributions to it.

STRUCTURE OF THE MEDIA INDUSTRIES

Chapter 2 analysed the industrialisation of the mass media, and their differentiation into large industrial organisations. The contemporary evolutionary stage was described there as one of concentration, and this section looks at the various aspects of this process. The variety of pressures on each of the media has produced three sorts of responses. Firstly companies have become integrated, and as part of the wider 'takeover boom' of the 1960s large numbers of media companies joined together into larger combines. Secondly, to spread risks into a wider range of products and facilitate cost reduction and economies of scale, the media industries have diversified into a series of related activities in the leisure and general industrial sectors. The third response is internationalisation, a multifaceted process by which British media have sought solutions to their problems overseas. Each of these three responses needs to be examined in slightly more detail.

48

Integration has taken two forms. First, media companies in one sector have joined together with companies producing the same commodity. Thus newspapers have steadily come into fewer hands throughout the twentieth century, the cinema chains have progressively lengthened, and book publishers have sought financial solace in combination. Table 3 shows the extent of this aspect of concentration by estimating the proportion of the market controlled by the top five companies in each sphere.

TABLE 3

Proportion of total market accounted for by the five leading Companies in each medium, 1972[14]

	%
National morning newspaper circulations	86
National Sunday newspaper circulations	88
Commercial television, % television homes served	73
Paperback books: % domestic production (estimate, 1971)	86
Mid-price LP records: % market	69
Cinema: % box office takings (top four circuits)	80

This process of horizontal integration is complemented by vertical integration, the extension by companies in one sphere of operations into other stages in production, such as the supply of raw materials or the organisation of distribution and retailing. For example the leisure combine EMI has interests in film production, exhibition and distribution, as well as in finance and artists. Reed International is another example of this tendency. Predominantly a wood pulp, paper, and related products corporation, in 1970 Reed merged with the International

Publishing Corporation, the leading British newspaper and magazine group who publish the *Daily Mirror,* the *Sunday Mirror,* and the *Sunday People.*

Diversification is a wider industrial phenomenon. To meet the problems each medium has had to face the larger companies have joined operations with firms in other parts of the leisure industry, and increasingly beyond it with firms involved in a variety of activities. This enables them to concentrate their activities in the healthier sectors while cushioning themselves against the worst effects of depression in others. Table 4 gives some examples of the diversified activities of a few of the larger media companies.

TABLE 4

% distribution of turnover among some media companies, 1972[1][5]

Companies	Broadcasting	Film/ Cinema	News- papers	Publishing	Other media/ Leisure	Other
EMI	7	15			55	23
Granada	36	6		6	40	12
Associated Television Corporation	48	23			28	1
Rank		27			43	30
Pearson Longman			56	39		5
Thomson			40	24	27	9

This table does not, of course, indicate the common ownership of media companies, for example shareholding by newspapers and others in commercial television and radio is widespread. The mechanisms by which integration and diversification are effected are basically of two kinds. The first is this simple ownership or shareholding. To document the extent of such links is beyond the task of the present book, but it is a necessary observation on the response of the media to rising costs, changing leisure patterns, advertising fluctuations and the myriad other hazards they face. The second method is interlocking directorships which often, though not always, accompany shareholding and personify the mutual representation of interests between media organisations. Two of the most familiar of such networks link firstly EMI, Thames Television and *The Times,* and secondly ATC (ATV etc.), Reed, Beaverbrook (the *Express*), News International (*The Sun, News of the World*), and London Weekend Television. In addition these two chains are linked by family ties.

Internationalisation is no new aspect of the British media. But many aspects of it have developed in direct response to the pressures described in Chapter 2. The first aspect is the growth of exports. Nearly half the books produced in Britain are exported. The international selling of television programmes is one of the world's boom industries. The BBC alone sells programmes to nearly 100 countries. Total programme sales abroad by British broadcasting organisations totalled anything up to 20,000 hours in 1971—72.[16] The rapid growth of markets for cultural products in the developing countries is an important factor here.

The second aspect of internationalisation is ownership by British media of foreign media companies. One legacy of empire is a string of British owned newspapers throughout the world, though, as in West Africa, indigenisation has been rapid, and is often an important priority after independence. The third aspect is the reverse of this; foreign, particularly American, ownership of British media. However, the retreat of American capital from the film industry, the frequent lack of success of American publishing interests who have been involved in British firms, and the enduring insularity of the British Press (despite the Australian Murdoch and the

Canadian Thomson) are important caveats against a general impression of 'Americanisation'. A slightly different aspect is the production of media materials for the overseas, especially American market. The television programme export drive, for example, has been mainly directed across the Atlantic. In all these ways the media have turned to international markets and media to resolve the problems of domestic change and insecurity.

These three aspects of concentration represent the second stage in the historical process outlined in the previous chapter. They indicate some of the contingencies of survival in the mass media, not all of which are rooted in economic organisation, of course, but many of which necessarily are.

ECONOMIC ORGANISATION AND SOCIAL ORGANISATION

How significant to a sociology of the media are these economic factors? The recognition that the media are industrial and commercial organisations prompts an immediate awareness that their organisation and culture will be related to their command of a number of resources. For example, size will affect the ability of a medium to indulge in certain types of activity. A large thriving newspaper can expand its overseas staff and its newsgathering activities generally. Television companies have to be cost conscious and aware that a play production may cost six or seven times as much per hour as a feature film or an imported film series.[17] The necessity to attract an audience or advertising is bound to introduce perimeters around decision-making, and sway different emphases in content and organisation.

Three representative controversies can illustrate the significance of the relationship between economic and social organisation in the media. Firstly, the case is argued that big, even semimonopolistic media are necessary to supply the fourth estate arm of communications with the resources and weight required for its watchdog role. Thus investigative journalism requires massive industrial backing to lend it significance, confidence, and the ability to scale the other commanding heights of the social structure. Against this is set the riposte that in expanding its armoury the fourth estate has joined the opposing army; in other words that it has itself become part of the complex of powerful institutions which it should be its primary duty to survey.

The second controversy starts at the notion that in the evolution of the media, or any other industry, popular success and thus aggrandizement are the due reward and proof of social utility. Thus newspapers die, television programmes are ignored and rejected, cinemas close, and books lie idle on shelves as unfortunate victims of a process which serves to retain the best by trial in the marketplace. Against this are raised two dissenting views. First the classic liberal regard that 'if all mankind were of one opinion, and only one person were of the contrary opinion, mankind would be no more justified in silencing that one person, than he, if he had the power, would be justified in silencing mankind'.[18] The second objection is that the systematic rejection of the unpopular is likely to exclude not random minority voices, but consistently those that particularly deserve an audience in view of their innovativeness, challenge, or powerlessness.

The third controversy directly relates the economics of concentration with the social organisation of communications. It includes the familiar plea that creativity and accountancy do not mix.[19] But it is also a broader concern that the full range of cultural products will remain only potential while economics play the role in their diffusion that they do now. The argument is essentially that between the concern for the number of media 'voices' or channels, and the alternative view which turns more to the ownership and control of such outlets than their multiplicity.

53

All such controversies relate the wider economic and organisational environments of the media to the routines and practices involved in their day-to-day operations. The next chapter describes some of these procedures and their meaning and significance for the communicators involved in them.

The communicators and media production   4

THE COMMUNICATORS

One of the great gaps in our knowledge about the mass media is the lack of detailed information about the communicators; the producers, writers, creators, executives, technicians, journalists and others whose decisions and ideas shape mass media output. Over the period surveyed in Chapter 2 the number of institutionalised intellectuals and entertainers comprising the work force in the communications industries has rapidly increased, but it remains difficult to estimate actual figures.

Census figures are certainly a preliminary if inadequate guide. But they do show that the joint category of 'authors, journalists, and related workers' increased from 19,086 in 1951 to 31,950 in 1966. The majority of these, of course, are the various sorts of journalists, totalling about 24,000. Of these only about 3,500 work on the national Press. Authors are even more indeterminate. The majority of writers have institutional bases either in the professions or increasingly in education, forming what Bradbury calls a 'literary salariat'.[1] Findlater estimated the total in 1963 as between 6,500 and 7,000, though in 1972 40 per cent had incomes not derived from their writing, and 56 per cent earned less than £500 a year from writing.[2] The number of broadcasters is equally elusive, but the BBC alone had a programme production staff of over 10,000 in 1973 (not including engineering staff).

The picture is complicated by the movement of personnel between the media. Many freelance in journalism or broadcasting, deploying their talents into whichever medium is buoyant and offers work, or using their base in one organisational context to produce for another, as for example, a sports journalist might 'ghostwrite' a footballer's autobiography. Movement between the media may dilute occupational commitment to a single organisation and encourage more general commitment to the craft or profession, or perhaps more individually to a career. But there is little evidence about the extent of such 'spiralism' within the media. A study of specialist journalists found that over a third earned more than £500 a year from freelance writing, though the higher status specialists had little need of such work as a weapon in establishing their autonomy from their employing organisation.[3]

The overall numbers of an occupational group may disguise the numbers most actively involved in a particular media activity. For example, there are about 1,600 members of the association which looks after the interests of television and screen writers. But probably less than a tenth of them write something like 90 per cent of the scripts ultimately put into production.

While the growth in numbers has been extremely rapid the pattern of recruitment into the creative professions has not altered quite as much. To a large extent ascription rather than achievement remains the major entry permit. Several studies of the origins of writers show them to be predominantly middle-class and male, though most such studies suffer from a necessary historical concentration on major writers whose works have survived. Laurenson, in a study of 170 writers born or deceased between 1860 and 1910 found that nearly a half went to 'Oxbridge', that the majority were from the professional middle class, and only a quarter were women.[4] Altick, taking a slightly longer period, found much the same distribution, with the twentieth-century decline of the commercial middle class as a breeding ground for writers, and a 'lengthening discrepancy between the author-class and the reader-class'.[5]

Journalists tend not to come from such exalted origins, though their roots are often in the minor professions. The fathers of Tunstall's specialist journalists had occupations 'heavily weighted towards administrative, educational and service occupations, with little representation of manufacturing or heavy industry'.[6] Specialists almost certainly can boast more formal education than the majority of journalists, and the proportion of the specialists who had gone on to higher education, one-third, is much higher than is probably the case for the occupation as a whole. The notion of journalism as a craft demanding apprenticeship rather than either general education or specialised training is a core feature of the belief system of British journalists, though one that has occasioned a great deal of debate in recent years. In a study of trainee journalists in 1969 Boyd-Barrett found that 'over half the students came from lower-middle and upper-middle white-collar backgrounds'.[7] Nearly half had gained minimum university entrance requirements while at school. It is possible, however, that a trainee group now will have had more formal education than journalists as a whole, though, as with other media professionals very little data on their background is available.

Formal recruitment through training and the acquisition of entry requirements is an increasing index of the professionalisation of media occupations. Schemes run by, for example, the National Council for the Training of Journalists (since 1955), and the growing number of film and television courses in further education colleges reflect the feeling that occupational training could usefully operate as a control over entry into media occupations. But this goal necessarily conflicts with the ideal that the qualities required for success in a creative occupation are innate or, at best, learnt 'on the job'. Coupled with the oversubscription for entry into the more glamorous media this conflict has curtailed the effectiveness and power of training schemes.

Personalised particularistic assessments still predominate in recruitment. Boyd-Barrett noted that 'the onus of entry is placed very much on the shoulders of the applicant — he must declare himself in face of the lack of systematic channels for such declaration . . . Many practising journalists and editors regard this lack of system as an advantage.'[8] The BBC has in recent years cut back its training schemes for production staff and says that 'a person who joins the BBC after acquiring professional experience is at no long-term disadvantage compared with the one who enters as a trainee'.[9]

Career patterns within the media vary greatly with the age and type of medium and its rate of growth. If a medium is growing rapidly (as in the wartime BBC or the first five years of commercial television) upward mobility will be rapid and security well established. In a declining medium, like the cinema, career patterns will be uncertain and will probably straddle more than one medium.

Age distributions will reflect these variations, though we have little data to confirm this. In provincial journalism junior reporters form a large part of the workforce. In 1967 almost 30 per cent of the membership of the National Union of Journalists were aged between sixteen and twenty-three.[10] On the other hand in 1969 only 32 per cent of national, i.e. 'Fleet Street', journalists were under forty.[11] However, the traditional career pattern from the provinces to Fleet Street is in all likelihood not as routine as is frequently asserted. Tunstall found that 'so lacking in an orderly career structure was journalism that only a minority of careers followed even this *provincial career* pattern at all closely'.[12]

Commitment may be to a career in one organisation, in one medium, or solely to self-advancement. Media jobs with strong occupational ideologies will tend to secure strong commitment. However, where career orientation is more general the job may be seen as instrumental, its glamour and contacts functional currency for transfer to other occupations. As Tunstall notes, journalism is a 'bridging occupation', especially into public relations. Another outlet is politics — in 1972 sixty-seven MPs had been journalists or writers prior to their entry into full-time politics, and thirty had backgrounds in broadcasting.[13]

Burns, in looking at vocational commitment in the BBC found that career structure had produced four clear age grades:

the pioneers of the 1920s; a second group who are associated with the years of expansion and the establishment of the BBC as a nationally and internationally important institution during the 1930s; the wartime group, who identify themselves with the Corporation as it was in that time of emergency and triumph; and those who came in, with, or after, television.[14]

Since that was written in 1964 a further age group based on the graduate entrants of the mid 1960s has probably emerged.[15]

The market situation of cultural producers is clearly dominated by the changing structures of the organisations within which they work. As creative individuals they are no longer autonomous, and their market situation has changed from independence via patronage to employment. The likely effect is that unstructured work situations have become routinised, and the aura of amateurism has shaded into that of the professional. As an ideal type this reflects the expansion of industrialised culture production from rare creativity to widespread competence.

The work situation of people in the media will vary greatly, depending on their degree of autonomy from an organisation and the extent to which their role is defined as a creative one. Several factors need to be taken into account. Firstly, even within the category of creative workers in an organisation there will normally be considerable role differentiation. On a newspaper, for example, reporters who gather news and subeditors who process it do substantially different tasks and will define their roles in quite different and even antagonistic terms. The ratio between the two types of journalist is a differentiating characteristic of individual newspapers, popular papers generally having a higher proportion of processors and of processing. In the same way television production is effected by a production team and studio crew, whose styles and routines of work may be quite different.[16] Role differentiation will produce differentiated commitment, to a small peer group rather than an organisation, or to a small section of the production process rather than the final completed artefact. In this sense it is possible to discern a continuum from 'executive commitment' to 'aesthetic commitment' which contains the varied goals of work within the media. This variation in commitment will reflect position in the organisational hierarchy, too, with executive commitment tending to increase among the higher echelons.

Another variation in work situation will derive from the group or individual nature of the work. Television production is typically a group activity, with two coordinated sets of people concerned with the creative and the technical sides of a programme. The demands of technology will coerce even the normally individualistic task of writing into a fairly regulated and defined routine. Newspaper reporting is generally more individualistic in practice. Much time is spent away from the newspaper office, and the irregularity and unpredictability of journalism are important parts of the occupation's mythology.

The size of the media industry is a further factor determining occupational differentiation and work situation. Segmented occupations, as in Tunstall's portrayal of journalism, are likely to lack a clear picture of themselves and encourage commitment to components of the product rather than the whole. A large organisation will also define roles according to their function for the organisation rather than for an ultimate cultural product. Growth can lead to devolution, but stress due to a changing financial or political climate may produce centralisation, a process many have claimed to observe in the BBC in the recent past. Growth will also proliferate work roles. Lane, in a study of publishing, has drawn attention to the increasingly common extra layers of executives found in publishing houses as the volume of publishing and the size of publishers have expanded.[17] Extra roles of this kind often facilitate reconciliation of otherwise competing goals, in this case of economic and editorial considerations.

Jarvie has described the division of labour in large-scale film production. He suggests that producers, writers, stars and technicians will each be trying to satisfy different goals in different ways. The producer is mainly concerned with scheduling and budgets, while the director is anxious to satisfy the aesthetic criteria of his peers.[18] This characterisation may be less accurate for the more recent spread of independent film-making by producer-directors. The essential differentiation of tasks, however, remains, and is one of the problems of the cinema. As Montagu has described it, writing, scripting, marketing, casting, assembly, editing, music and so on are the work of specialists, best used in continuous production. But 'the casualisation of labour associated with irregular production defeats the purpose of economy',[19] and is thus one further symptom and cause of the decline of the cinema.

All these factors, then, impinge on the work situation of media personnel. The extent of role differentiation, organisational size, individual autonomy, group or individual production, all shape the nature of media work. One central problem running through all these factors is the opposition of creativity and control.

CREATIVITY AND CONTROL

All organisations involved in the production of culture are faced with a persistent dilemma. They must find ways of reconciling their organisational needs for regularity, routine, control, and even survival, with the commitment of creators to their skills or craft. The organisation must somehow accommodate the luxuries of unstructured unpredictability which are claimed by creators. The belief in the freedom of creativity is, of course, partly the legacy of Romanticism; an idealisation functional for the explanation of failure or for conflict with bureaucracy rather than an accurate description of how media production occurs. It nevertheless affects the relations of media producers with the organisations.

What then are the controls being contested? Firstly the creator is not the arbiter of his own product. His ideas have to be tailored for and judged by organisational demands, whether it is the formula of a television drama series, the style and tone of a newspaper, or the technical demands of film production. This means he must fit into an authority structure where executive demands overrule creative ones, though the two may often be closely related. Both short-term decisions about the suitability and amendment of existing work, and longer-term decisions about what is to be produced derive from such executive demands. The omnipresence of authority is tersely captured in a BBC injunction as expressed by the managing director: 'the wrath of the Corporation in its varied human manifestations is particularly reserved for those who fail to refer.'[20] This relates to the established BBC policy of referral upwards, in which all decisions are to be taken or at least approved at that level in the hierarchy ultimately responsible for them.

A second control is implicit in job delimitation. News gatherers seldom see their product in print as they have written it, television and film scripts have to be integrated with production techniques, and so on. The corollary of the division of labour in media production is segmented commitment and task specification. This acts as a control on creativity, which ideally is concerned with a completed process from conception through production to dissemination, by reducing its scope.

A third set of controls is ideological. Media organisations often evolve an ethos of what is accepted and appropriate which is learnt by newcomers, and included in their own evaluation and planning of their work. This is frequently mentioned in connection with the BBC, as 'a general view of what is fitting and seemly, of what is admissible and not admissible, which is gradually absorbed by those persons involved in programme-making'.[21] In a slightly less mystical way a journalist learns a paper's policy, not merely its overt political stance but its standard treatment of recurrent topics. He learns by reading the paper, through organisational lore, through the mechanism of career, and to a lesser extent in formal training. Inevitably he is drawn to, and feels happier in, newspapers with an ethos he can accept. This matching of attitudes has been coyly described by one proprietor as a 'happy coincidence',[22] but one can assume it is not uniformly coincidental, nor sufficiently efficient to be totally happy. Here again, however, control on creativity is effected not by malign suppression so much as work routine, anticipatory self-discipline, and occupational tradition.

Because innovation and imagination are central elements in the creator's ideology they have to be licensed by organisations, but within strong definitional boundaries. This ambiguity is seen in film genres, or in the writing of television series where stock characters are used in new plots. Formula production is in large part an economic demand, facilitating the location and capture of an audience. Elliott has written of the chains of familiar subjects, presentation routines, and personal contacts which cause 'a new production [to draw] on the established culture of the media, thus ensuring similarity and continuity in the view of the world presented'.[23]

A fourth control on creativity is that based on limitations of resources, both tangible in the form of money and equipment, and intangible in the form of information and time. In television, programme budgeting controls both sorts of resources; for example, both the amount of filming that can be done and the time available for research. The implications of financial stringency were touched on in Chapter 2, but as a control on the individual creator they are indirectly channelled through the organisation.[24] For example, in television they lead to formula production and less expensive or unpopular programmes, in newspapers to fewer pages and less expenditure on news gathering.

Time can rank highly in the conscious limitations of a media practitioner. One Fleet Street editor has even written that 'of all the pressures operating on the editor of a morning or evening newspaper the heaviest is the shortage of time'.[25] Television journalists are often aware that a full news bulletin may contain less verbal material than even one page of a serious newspaper. The pressures on selection of news items are amplified by the time factor, as well as other technical and occupational demands.

Finally, creativity is subject to a variety of formal controls. Like many other controls the law acts as much through anticipatory self-censorship as through retrospective litigation. The laws relating to libel, official secrets, obscenity, and so ón, all have an impact on daily media production. Organisations produce their own interpretations and procedures for protecting their creative staff and thereby themselves.

All these limitations on creativity produce responses which attempt to evade or loosen them. Two sorts of responses are common. Either an occupational ideology evolves which explains away the controls or in other ways buttresses the creator's self-image. Alternatively the work situation is manipulated to minimise the controls, or at least to lessen the discomfort they produce. These two responses need not be exclusive, but we can consider them separately.

An occupational ideology is the set of ideas an occupational group uses to explain the meaning and nature of the work to members of the group, and also to outsiders. Creative occupations usually have strong occupational ideologies, especially when working in organisations places them on the defensive. Many elements of the ideology are responses to organisational control. Firstly, many communicators practise distancing, a professional cynicism about their product which demeans the job while at the same time implying that the creator both perceives the deficiencies and is talented enough to transcend them. Journalists tend to rank the status of their occupation fairly low, an image with roots in Grub Street, the idea of 'hack' writing and disdain for the seedier tasks of reporting. Carr-Saunders and Wilson, writing in 1933 of the professional aspirations of journalists, considered that the 'onerous and responsible task of ascertaining the truth about current events . . . has fallen under the sway of men with the manners and morals of vendors of quack medicines'.[26] With such public disdain self-respect is reasserted by distancing from the job role.

A second element is segmented commitment, the belief that whatever the defects of the organisation's product, the creator's contribution is adequate. Thus the communicator will seek pride in the story not the newspaper, the individual programme rather than the output of a television company as a whole. Within the BBC Burns discerned a major trio of commitments to work, department and career. But he was able to trace a further variety of commitments to the work group, the studio, the age group, to diffuse attractions in the prestige and glamour of broadcasting, and so on.[27]

A third strand in the occupational ideology is to identify the creative group with broader goals, professional, ethical or political. Many media jobs involving writing can be seen by their practitioners as the work of constrained intellectuals whose larger commitment to writing as a skill is shackled by the confines of immediate demand. The idea of special technical competence and debates about professionalisation in the media are attempts to retain status in situations where changing values are placed on new skills. In a slightly different way 'political' constraints on journalism are accompanied by a commitment to the notions of objectivity and impartiality, though the actual practices associated with these values derive very largely from changes in journalism in the second half of the nineteenth century.

Specialisation adds a fourth element to the occupational ideology. The elaboration of ever more esoteric skills encourages a specialised argot, an air of 'insiderness', and is a powerful weapon in the battle against organisational control. Just as studies of scientists in industry show their commitment to their own specialisation and the community of scientists, so communicators can involve themselves in a range of outside affiliations providing new sources of status and professional association. Tunstall's study of specialist journalists show how their elite competence provides a widespread reputation among and involvement with extra-organisational peers which sustain autonomy from the employing organisation.

A fifth ideological response is alienation, a supposed result of frustrated creativity. Bradbury, writing of the 'literary salariat', even suggests that the commercialisation of creative writing has gone so far that the modern writer is not sufficiently alienated.[28] As a response to limitations on creativity expressions of alienation serve to distance the communicator from his work and reinforce the belief that its shortcomings are no fault of his own. In the larger commercial entertainments it is the business nature of his work that is seen by the communicator as alienating, and thus his occupational ideology expresses distaste and resignation over his situation.

Finally, occupational ideologies can be limitations on creativity in themselves. Journalism relies on 'news values', an acquired sense of those events which are newsworthy and the ways in which they are to be treated. These values can become 'inferential structures' which shape the perception of events into preconceived patterns based on previous experience of parallel events. A study by Halloran *et al* of coverage of an anti-Vietnam war demonstration in 1968 showed how a largely peaceful rally was in fact portrayed, both before and after the event, as a violent confrontation paralleling police-demonstrator battles earlier in the year in Chicago and Paris.[29]

The second means of responding to control is by manipulation of the work situation to reduce the uncertainty of organisational authority. Specialist journalists do this by 'competitor colleagueship', informal exchanges between specialists in the same area working for different news organisations. This goes beyond formal association in groups. Of the journalists studied by Tunstall 23 per cent belonged to cooperative partnerships, and an even higher proportion were aware of partnerships elsewhere in their specialism.[30]

Another mode of manipulating the work situation is the reassertion of independence, commonly by freelancing. This has been a growing form of employment in broadcasting since the introduction of commercial television. Elliott points out that it can lead to diminished power on the part of creators, but 'it also has the opposite effect of limiting the range of sanctions which an executive producer can bring to bear on a producer, or a producer on other members of a production team.'[31] Not only can creative personnel obtain independence from a single organisation by freelancing but it also facilitates operating in more than one medium. The main overlap is between television and the cinema, but a similar manipulation of autonomy is exercised by journalists who write books or provide material for other newspapers (provincial journalists for the nationals, for example).

The greatest assertion of autonomy is achieved by the independent creator, who can occupy a totally diffuse creative role, though largely dependent on others for the entrepreneurial roles attached to communications. Very few, however, are in this category except a minority of writers or high prestige performers able to exchange their commercial potential for the indulgence of autonomous decision-making.

While these various problems of controls on creativity, and the various ways of diminishing them are important, it is necessary not to overstate this. Many of these conflicts are made latent by the internalisation of organisational or other non-professional goals. Some other restraints on communicators come from less direct sources, however, in their relationships to other groups like peers and audiences.

THE COMMUNICATORS AND THEIR AUDIENCE

The communicators' attitudes to their audiences will be shaped by three factors; their knowledge about the audience, their social relationships with the audience, and the degree to which reception of media output is necessarily taken into account in creating that output. The defining characteristic of mass communications is that the audience is large, anonymous, and passive. To a large extent the communicator can have no knowledge of the impact of his products.

McQuail has suggested four reactions that result from this uncertainty: paternalism, specialisation, professionalism, and ritualism.[32] Paternalism, the assumption that ignorance of the audience is no hindrance to providing for it, can take both patrician and demotic forms either as an elitist notion of purposive uplift or as commercial pandering to a lowest common denominator. Specialisation and professionalism are part of the same process, and both encourage the use of peer groups as reference groups. Elliott noted that while the programme-makers he studied received a few letters, 'in many ways isolation and autonomy were the most striking characteristics of the production team's situation',[33] and they relied largely on their own reactions and that of colleagues to judge the programmes they had made. Burns, however, in his study of the BBC, found producers isolated even from each other, in what he describes as a world of 'autistic activity and belief' in which 'the professional role of television or radio producer requires him to insulate himself . . . from the worlds of other productions, both his own past efforts and those proceeding concurrently.'[34]

Professionalism can lay claim to an abstract and implicit code of ethics, as in the journalistic credo of objectivity, impartiality and accuracy. Responsibility to the audience may be an important part of such an ethic. In a study of television producers covering the 1966 election campaign Blumler found that this sense of responsibility was expressed both in terms of a felt need to serve the audience by making the election interesting, and in reference to professional judgment about the relative importance of issues using standards independent of the priorities of politicians.[35]

Ritualism involves reliance on well-tried formulae, a safety first procedure aimed more at keeping an existing audience than gaining a new one. While obviously a response to the sort of ignorance about the audience described by McQuail, this is also a response to broader pressures on the economics of the media. Thus newspapers aim to create a loyal readership able to identify with their style and opinions. In a similar way television series often adopt thematic titles for play sequences to encourage regular viewing. A separate aspect of formula production is the frequent use of the same media performers, not merely proven professionals but select outsiders whose ability to communicate makes them recurrently desirable. Elliott constructs a continuum of use from the comparatively invisible unknown 'ordinary citizen' to the media 'stars', the highly visible and regularly exposed 'global thinkers' on whom television in particular relies.[36]

The nature of concern about the audience will vary with knowledge about its reactions and about its demands.

Audience research is largely an attempt to predict the latter on the basis of the former. All major media organisations conduct audience research of one sort of another, and a large industry is based on this research. In aggregate the two broadcasting organisations spend almost £1 million a year on audience research, and one estimate of all commercial, administrative and service research of a simple head-counting type conducted in Britain arrived at a figure of at least £3 million in 1969.[37] Although the object is usually to find out how many people read a given newspaper or watch a television programme, advertisers and sales managers like also to know to what sorts of people they are marketing their products. But how do *communicators,* use this information?

Of Tunstall's correspondents, 34 per cent saw audience research figures, but most had a general indifference to them. This may have partly explained interesting misconceptions about their readers. When asked about the social composition of their audience the correspondents consistently and considerably underestimated the proportion of manual working-class readers. Television executives are frequently caricatured as impatiently pacing in weekly anticipation of the ratings on which their livelihoods depend. But the figures may be for reassurance rather than information. As McQuail remarks, 'the very regularity and predictability of findings about the audience may lessen their significance for the communicator'.[38] Burns, in his study of the BBC, speaks of a 'reluctance to disturb a complex of assumptions about the relationships of the BBC to its functions and to the public'.[39] Yet at the same time, he found attempts to explain away audience research findings when they were examined (by reference to unusual circumstances surrounding a particular broadcast), which he describes as 'rather like watching the whole practice of medicine being reduced to the use of the thermometer'.[40]

Communicators also rely for their knowledge of the audience on such sections of it as they meet in their daily lives. Relations, friends, taxi drivers, doormen, and secretaries serve as functional microcosms of the unknown audience, and are frequently mentioned in defence against the accusation that communicators are too isolated from and unresponsive to their audiences. This is not the direct feedback of, say, theatre audiences, so much as instant polling. Necessarily, of course, just like writers of letters to newspapers, or contributors to 'phone-in' broadcasts, this immediate response is unrepresentative of the wider audience.

Routine broadcasts receive very few direct audience reactions in the form of letters or telephone calls, and these have little impact. The correspondence received by the programme team studied by Elliott 'was no use to the production team in suggesting programme ideas for the future, because of its content, the way the team reacted to it, and because by the time most of it arrived, the production team had disbanded and each member was working with another team on a new programme'.[41] Tunstall's correspondents received an average of fourteen letters a week each, but many were 'crank' letters, factual enquiries, or otherwise unhelpful in giving information about the readers. Nonetheless such letters were the specialists' 'most regular experience of members of the general audience'.[42] A former Controller of BBC Television has written about this sort of contact:

> If one works in television one must reconcile oneself to the fact that the bulk of audience reaction is from cranks, from the unstable, the hysterical and sick . . . To form an equable judgement about one's audience from phone calls or correspondence is difficult if not impossible . . . The only positive thing the programme-maker knows about its audience is its size.[43]

Given this ignorance, communicators are forced to judge by their immediate peers and other close contacts. Austin

Mitchell has argued that this is particularly true in current affairs television, because of the uniform origins of producers who 'too often assume they are doing programmes for people very much like themselves'.[44] A study by Noble of producers making programmes for children asked them to predict the response of children to various parts of a programme. To a large degree the producers did fairly badly in assessing how well children understood the programme.[45] This is an audience removed from the communicators by the extra dimension of age, which not only makes them unlike the communicators, but also reinforces their exclusion from the voicing of opinions and shaping of decisions about material provided for them. To circumvent the gap between audiences and communicators a growing demand for access to the media has come from a variety of interest groups. Such access as has been granted, however, is by licence rather than as an institutionalised component of mass communication.

Communicators' ignorance of audiences is thus treated in four ways. It is accepted as the necessary corollary of mass communications. It is treated functionally as the liberation of professional judgment from the tyranny of the marketplace. It is deemed unfortunate but redeemable by reference to a notional representative audience composed of peers and other contacts. Finally, attempts are made to minimise the problem either by better research or by more direct access, though neither of the latter ploys has greatly reduced the gulf.

Communicators have more diffuse relationships with their audiences in direct, non-professional social contacts. These will be members of the audience 'accidentally', rather than as the main facet of their relationship with the communicator. However, as with many occupations which spill over into non-work time, media occupations tend to enclose the private lives of their practitioners, encircling the social contacts and contexts within which their leisure is spent.

Because of this the communicator can be seen within three

spheres of indirect social contact. First there are the 'special' audiences with whom he has regular contact but who are not themselves communicators. Journalists, for example, deal with regular news sources, and creators in most media meet professional critics irregularly. These people provide respected, or at least influential, reaction to the communicator's work, as well as being repositories of significant and relevant information and lore and matters of common professional concern. The second sphere is that comprising the circle of friends and intimates with whom the communicator associates. Because communicators tend to be more affluent, more middle-class and better educated than their audiences, this sphere is unlikely to be representative of these audiences. In addition the irregular and unusual hours of work of many communicators tend not only to make social contact outside difficult, but also reinforce the tendency to mix largely with colleagues and people in the profession. This is especially true for journalists; over 40 per cent of the three best friends of the group studied by Tunstall were also journalists.[46]

Professionalism, irregularity, a strong occupational culture, well developed informal communications and spillover work-leisure patterns, all can be found to some extent in many occupations; it is their common coincidence in communications that separates the communicators from their audiences. The third sphere of contact, that of the general public, is therefore the least available to the communicator. Communicators and audiences do not normally have similar characteristics and attitudes, though they may have, especially in minority media. Whether this matters, whether they should be closer, or whether wider access to communications could obviate the problem altogether, are questions to be framed in wider perspectives on the mass media than can be tackled here.

ORGANISATIONAL AND OTHER GOALS

Media organisations and the communicators may have different objectives. A basic confrontation is that already described between the economic or bureaucratic goals of the organisation and the professional or creative goals of the communicator. Most studies of communicators mentioned in this chapter touch on this conflict. Tunstall, for example, divides organisational goals into revenue and non-revenue goals. Lane, in his study of publishers, discovered role conflict between what he terms economic and cultural goals, and between the function of serving the author and serving the public.[47] It is possible that in a declining small publisher adherence to cultural goals and rejection of purely economic ones is making a virtue of necessity.

A similar model can be detected in television production. Three dominant sets of goals face a programme-making organisation. Within a broad set of *economic goals* which closely affect all others, *organisational goals* and *professional goals* also determine the shape of programme output. Audience maximisation is a major economic goal for which entertainment criteria have to be met, so that success is registered firstly in the ratings, and in the case of the commercial companies in the likelihood of networking. Organisational goals can derive from this relationship with the network, with controlling bodies like the IBA, or with external legal, cultural, political and economic demands. The organisation must coordinate all its output in an overall strategy controlling costing, personnel policy and general treatment of any single production.

Professional goals attach to programmes and to personnel. To fulfil them programmes must make 'good television' and satisfy criteria many of which derive from the strong show business pedigree in television, and are as diffuse and inexplicit as they are ubiquitous. Personal professional goals relate to career patterns in television and the criteria of success erected by traditions and trade lore on the one hand,

74

and by current power holders on the other, as well as to the occupational community and broader personal commitments of a political, artistic or ethical nature.

To reconcile the goals of communicators and organisations the former frequently organise, especially in response to rapid change and the perception of threat to an occupation. The Society of Authors, formed in 1883, was a response to the decreasing rewards of writing and the growing power of the publishers. Though despised by some, like the writer George Gissing to whom the society was 'a mere gathering of tradesmen', it has survived as an organisation willing to fight vociferously for better financial rewards for writers, despite small membership and lack of representativeness.

The National Association of Journalists was formed in 1884 and is a good example of the dual functions of such organisations. Unionisation was long opposed in journalism for status reasons, the professional aspirations of many journalists combining with their occupational individualism and white-collar snobbery. When association did come it was 'rather a desire to copy the organisation of established professions than any spontaneous movement towards coalescence'.[48] The Association became the Institute of Journalists in 1890 and continued to concentrate on professional goals of standards, training and status. Poor wages and conditions, especially in the provinces, were untouched by these concerns, and as the official history describes it, a trifle theatrically, 'to these starveling scribes scattered all over the country came the call to fight for economic justice'.[49] The National Union of Journalists arose in Manchester in 1907 and dealt almost exclusively with pay and conditions, enforcing a national minimum wage agreement in 1919 and joining the TUC in 1926. Its membership rapidly outgrew the Institute's and it is now the much larger organisation. Intermittent attempts at reconciliation have failed and the different aims and characters of the organisations persist.

A similar dichotomy of aims is found in organisations in the other media. The growth of broadcasting created a host of new occupations, mostly within a single organisation. This produced the additional dilemma, common in white-collar service occupations, of the choice between staff and occupational organisation. The BBC Staff Association was formed at the beginning of World War II and by 1949 included 46 per cent of the staff, especially in the regions and in long-term occupations. But heterogeneity of occupations kept membership low, though it was above average among programme staff.[50] The coming of commercial television re-emphasised the dilemma and indirectly led to the formation of an Association of Broadcasting Staff, though this has never become industrywide. It is not recognised by the commercial companies but includes roughly 50 per cent of BBC employees and the same proportion of the IBA itself; a membership of about 11,000 altogether.

One vestige of the difference between the ABS and the unions is the greater industrial virility of the latter (though a strike by the ABS in 1969 has sometimes been seen as a break in the cosy relationship with the BBC). Those unions which, while deriving from occupations outside broadcasting have many members within the medium, are joined in a Federation of Broadcasting Unions, which itself is not recognised by the IBA for negotiations;[51] the BBC also has always preferred negotiation with the staff association. In the early years of commercial television shortage of trained staff and studio accommodation led to a reliance on films and film personnel. This in turn led to large-scale representation by film unions like the National Association of Theatrical and Kiné Employers, which latterly acquired an extra 'T' in its acronym to accommodate the newer medium. The cinema already had a more specific organisation, the Association of Cinematograph and Allied Technicians, dating from 1933, which has similarly modified its title to include television, and now has about 16,000 members.

Apart from such formal organisations communicators have had frequent recourse to informal association in *ad hoc* pressure groups of various kinds. These can reflect dissatisfaction with the formal organisations, much as the NUJ expressed the dissatisfaction of many provincial journalists with the IOJ, or be rumblings of discontent with the organisation of the medium. Various ginger groups within broadcasting have developed as new technologies and the likelihood of impending reorganisation have been discussed. Some of these have specific aims, like the demands of 'the 76 Group' for an inquiry into broadcasting prior to the renewal of the BBC's Charter and the Television Act in 1976. Others have more general objectives like the Free Communications Group which believed in radically restructuring the ownership, control and organisation of all media. A final strategy has been production outside the established media. The 'underground' Press is an example of this, though never as flourishing in recent years as in the first quarter of the nineteenth century, or as widespread in Britain as in the USA.

In this chapter we have looked at the communicators and the way they relate to the media within which they work. The next step is to examine the relationships between the media and other organisations and institutions.

The media and the social system 5

It is meaningless to discuss any social institution such as mass communications as though it operated in isolation, unconnected to other social processes. The media are central in the provision of ideas and images which people use to interpret and understand a great deal of their everyday experience. They therefore relate to other institutions both structurally, through organisational ties and interaction, and culturally, by conveying information and impressions about society. This chapter examines the nature and importance of these relationships.

THE MEDIA AND THE POLITICAL SYSTEM

In most advanced industrial societies the mass media are an integral part of political life, though not as centrally as once prophesied by Lord Northcliffe, who believed that 'the independent newspaper will be one of the future forms of government'. In some senses he was right, however, in that for most people the media provide their major or only link with government as well as the information on which political judgments and attitudes are based. Most communicators are convinced of these generalisations. A former Director-General of the ITA has written that 'without newspapers and without broadcasting modern self-government simply could not work at all'.[1] Politicians are equally aware of the increasing political role of the media; the declining importance of party manifestos is sometimes cited as an index of this.

There are two complementary ways of approaching political communications. Firstly the timespan to be considered can be the immediate or short-term, or the long-term persistent communication of political information. Secondly, the communication can be overtly and purposively political, with deliberate intent to persuade, or it can be only incidentally political. These two possibilities are schematically represented in Figure 1.

Fig. 1

| | | Timespan | |
		long-term	short-term
political intent	purposive	policy	campaigns
	non-purposive	ideology	inferential structures

Research has predomiminantly looked at election campaigns or the effects of proprietorial policy on media content. Belatedly, the study of inferential structures or 'unwitting bias' has become part of the increasing amount of research on journalism.[2] Least considered, because most difficult to analyse and describe, is the ideological nature of communications, the unintentional import of underlying structural interests into mass media content.

It is possible to summarise the main findings of research on the media and election campaigns. Firstly electors appear to acquire new information during the campaign about the issues, parties, and personalities involved, but attitudes to these things vary much less. Any changes in attitudes and information are proportional to the extent of exposure to campaign material in the media. Trenaman and McQuail, in their study of the 1959 election campaign, found that there was a 'lack of any widespread reaction in the population as a whole to the mass of relevant material to which they are exposed during the election campaign',[3] and that those least exposed to media material acquired very little new information germane to the election.

A second general research finding is the low persuadibility of the majority of electors. Selective perception concentrates attention and trust on those messages already accepted. Three-quarters of the audience for party political broadcasts, for example, are normally composed of sympathisers to the party concerned. However, reinforcement is not universal; research by the Leeds Centre for Television Research on the 1964 election concluded that reinforcement of existing political attitudes 'occurs selectively among those who look for it or whose prior attitudes towards the content of a communication encourage a reinforcing result'.[4]

Thirdly, throughout the history of electoral television audiences for political broadcasting have remained high. Actual journalistic coverage on television of elections only began with the 1959 campaign, but the parties had become convinced of the efficacy of party political broadcasting much earlier, and 'there was no aspect of their electoral tactics in 1950 to which they gave more thought or care'.[5] Though receiving slightly lower audience figures that year than in 1945, in 1951 at least some of the broadcasts were heard by 82 per cent of the electorate. Television in 1951 reached less than 10 per cent, however, and party political broadcasts were merely repeats in sound only at the end of the day of the earlier radio programmes.[6] By 1959 television ownership had shot up and 61 per cent of the electorate saw at least one party political broadcast.[7] Reporting of elections was still muted, but in 1964 14 per cent of peak time output on BBC1 was devoted to the election.[8] In recent elections audiences for party political broadcasts have been roughly a quarter of the population, and coverage in current affairs has increased.

A fourth research interest has been in the characteristics of those voters who do change their intention as a result of exposure to the media. Some findings suggest that rather than being the knowledgeable voter who attends assiduously and weighs the party campaign rationally, the changer is likely to be low in political motivation and lacking in information.

> In a situation where much television viewing arises from habit, and where the political content of the medium is suddenly enlarged by the launching of an election campaign, the group most likely to undergo a substantial increase in exposure to political communications will consist of those individuals who would not normally seek out political programmes.[9]

The earlier Leeds study suggested that in 1959 changers were not very different from others, but if anything rather better informed and motivated. Overall, however, the study found 'a definite and consistent barrier' between media exposure and attitude change during the campaign. In the slightly longer term the media may affect the changing drift of partisanship, especially among the uncommitted. In the most important study of electoral choice conducted in this country, Butler and Stokes found that between 1964 and 1966 73 per cent of their panel of respondents had shifted their opinions towards the party supported by the newspaper they read, and 27 per cent had actually changed party allegiance to that of their newspaper's. They cautiously concluded that 'we may therefore attribute to the Press some role in changing the relative strength of the parties in the short run as well as in forming and conserving more enduring allegiances'.[10]

A fifth conclusion from electoral research is that the media are used for general impressions rather than specific information or images. The uses made by people of media output during election campaigns were extensively examined in the 1964 Leeds research. They found that the campaign was followed diligently by enthusiasts both of politics and television. General surveillance, that is gathering of political information to keep in touch with affairs, was important to over half their respondents whereas party broadcasts were used for vote guidance by 26 per cent. The excitement of the contest was a third attraction for a proportion of the audience.[11] The arousal of interest and active involvement in information-seeking at election periods may be more to do with the uncustomary awareness of the possibility of political action by the voter — his acquiescence is being solicited after all — than a result of the power of television.

This diffuse use of the media reflects the similar finding that the media focus issues rather than sway intentions directly. A small list of major topics is crystallised by the media as the essence of each campaign: nationalisation and prices in 1951, immigration, strikes in 1964, and so on. The media thus emphasise the issues on which the campaign devolves and to which politicians have to address themselves. By venting areas not normally much exposed the media may significantly alter perceptions of the political scene. In the 1964 election the comparative success of the Liberals has been partly explained as an artifact of the unaccustomed attention paid to them by the media, reassuring voters of their presence and viability.[12] This is an instance of the general phenomenon of 'status conferral' by which appearance in the media enhances personalities and organisations to which attention is given.

Sixthly, the relationship between television and the Press in election coverage has gradually changed, as the newer medium has gathered a larger audience and lost some of the inhibitions and legal constraints which formerly controlled political broadcasting. In 1950 there were no television election broadcasts and the BBC 'kept as aloof from the election as if it had been occurring on another planet'.[13] Despite this the Press, in one writer's estimation, did not succeed 'in gaining the attention and control of public opinion to anything like the extent that certain newspapers did in the 1924, 1931, or even 1945 election'.[14] By 1959 television was dominant and newspapers were increasingly turning to opinion polling for election news. Television is consistently ranked by the majority as the most reliable and useful source for political information. By the 1974 election the campaign had become effectively its coverage on television, with concomitant complaints that a debate was being reduced to a spectacle.

Finally, analysis of media output during elections has shown a growing tendency to 'presidentialise' elections, and to focus on the central personalities and leaders. Fears that this leads to triviality and playing to the gallery are countered by Blumler's assertion, in discussing this argument, that 'most voters probably appreciate the difference between show business and political activity'.[15] Harrison has calculated that in both 1966 and 1970 53 per cent of the news time devoted to all politicians during the campaigns was about the two main party leaders. He found that in 1970, of the 1,837 candidates only 44 were mentioned in broadcast bulletins.[16]

All these empirical generalisations about the media and politics describe the short-term purposive communications earlier labelled campaigns. But this may not be the most significant impact of the media on the political system. Blumler has argued that 'the vote as such was always an unpromising focus of any attempt to trace the political power of the mass media'.[17] Butler and Stokes found that only 11 per cent of the electorate changed their voting intention during the 1966 campaign; for the majority partisanship is a lifetime commitment rather than a rationally considered choice every few years. It is more likely that the media 'set the agenda' for political debate. They define the boundaries within which people think about and discuss political issues, and provide the symbols and explanations with which these issues are articulated. Thus the media mould public opinion, and indeed to a great extent media output *is* public opinion, or at least the most accessible index of what commentators conventionally refer to as public opinion. One influential theory has described a 'two-step flow' of communications, in which media material is attended to most actively by an interested and aware elite, called opinion leaders, who then pass it on through networks of interpersonal communications.[18] These interpersonal networks stabilise attitudes over time and act as filters for mediated information. Of course, there is a paradox in this formulation in that both opinion leaders and those they lead receive their information from the media, though in different degrees and contexts.

> Those who are in the habit of talking about politics with family and friends do not constitute a separate, isolated part of the British culture. On the contrary, the information which the voter receives in communications of this sort will normally have had its origin in the mass media, even though it may have undergone various transformations along the way.[19]

In the short term public opinion may be stirred or moulded almost entirely by the mass media, particularly as a result of campaigns or purposive attempts to rouse feelings on issues where public knowledge may be minimal or dormant. The campaign to raise money for thalidomide children in 1972–73 was an example of this. The long-term impact is more complex. Despite the widespread Press support for entry into the EEC, opinion polls through the 1960s showed a large minority confused by the whole issue and, in the later years, a growing opposition to entry.[20] The entire notion of public opinion is most commonly framed in terms of 'the public's' attitude to specific questions of policy, whereas the probable effect of the media is on broader beliefs and attitudes to non-specific political concerns. Most generally the long-term political importance of the media is more likely to derive from non-purposive, ideological communication. In portraying the predominantly accepted forms of power relationships in society, and legitimating means of reconciling conflicts of interest which are themselves part of those relationships, the media are an important contributor to the maintenance of societal consensus. The short-term changes studied in electoral research are in this respect only of secondary significance. One field of research that has looked at the longer term is that concerned with the acquisition of political awareness by children.

Political attitudes tend to be stable through the life cycle and appear to relate strongly to political socialisation within the family. Both partisanship and interest in politics have been traced to family origins, but by and large little research has been conducted on the sources of children's political information and beliefs. The usual approach has concentrated on the development of such attitudes through the life cycle rather than their origins. The media are central among these origins. Recent research by Elizabeth Eyre-Brook found that, while teenagers are not heavy television viewers, 73 per cent of the eleven- to fifteen-year-olds in her sample saw television almost every day.[21] For many pre-adolescents the media form a major part of their leisure activities. They are also cited as the major source of information about general affairs in the world. In Eyre-Brook's study 85 per cent named television as their main source for information generally, a long way ahead of school, the family, and friends. There are two qualifications to this. Firstly, the media have their main impact on levels of information rather than attributes; thus statement about sources, which will inevitably be framed with information in mind, will stress the media. Secondly, since information gain will be greatest on topics about which little is known the general finding must be explored for more specific uses. Thus Eyre-Brook found that information about government was gathered by her respondents largely from television, whereas parents were the main source of information on a specific political area like voting. Local newspapers were the main source of information about jobs. Generally the topics where information is mostly gleaned from the media will be those most remote from children's everyday experience.

Understanding of trade unions, for example, among those children whose everyday experience gave them some direct information about unions, was quite different from the views of those children who relied on the media. While for most children there was little awareness of unions except in the context of strikes, of those whose main sources were the media 50 per cent had very low knowledge of related issues like the purposes of unions or what they are, whereas of those whose sources were more direct only 23 per cent had similar difficulty.

Foreign countries and peoples are also unfamiliar to most children. An early study by Himmelweit found that after one year of exposure to the new medium of television children are more likely to know about aspects of foreigners' lives rather than make simple evaluations, but that this knowledge was largely framed by the stereotypical presentations in television fiction.[22] In a study of children's reading of comics Johnson discovered that regular readers were more nationalistic than non-readers, in much the same simplistic xenophobic way as their comics.[23]

One problem in this area is that 'the existing evidence is largely about feelings for and against countries and peoples and there is little to show whether early orientations to the political system, or conceptual development, are affected'.[24] By defining such topics as non-political it becomes a self-fulfilling prophecy that the relationship between the media and political socialisation will remain uncertain. In suggesting the most important problems they felt faced Britain in 1971 Eyre-Brook's respondents named the Common Market, the cost of living, and strikes. All these have obvious political connotations, and their selection and ranking is itself a political evaluation reflecting media output quite closely.

This wider view brings us to a more general perspective on the media and the political system. The media operate in the political system by conveying information. Seymour-Ure has elaborated on this idea by suggesting a distinction between horizontal communication between members of the 'political public' whose activities the media describe, and vertical communication to the 'mass public' for whom the information is provided.[25] Members of the political elite may themselves use the media as a primary source about the activities of their peers, and this may be one side effect of specialised political administration. Barker and Rush, in a study of how Members of Parliament acquire information, demonstrate the importance of weekly journals and local newspapers to this special audience. They found, however, that MPs' media use is very different from that of their constituents, particularly in their low exposure to television.[26] Official use of the media for information about foreign countries has increased in the wake of reorganised diplomatic representation. A government report in 1969 suggested that 'very little political reporting [by diplomatic posts] of any kind is needed in modern conditions ... given the amount of international news and comment which is already available in London through the Press and other public media'.[27]

In addition to this passive role the media may take an active part in politics. Seymour-Ure has described how the timing and nature of Press revelations about the Profumo affair in 1963 were key elements in the ensuing events.[28] A similar contribution can be made less intentionally, as in the Cabinet reshuffle of 1962 when reports of impending changes precipitated their occurrence.[29] Such isolated incidents are important elements in the mythology of political potency maintained by the media and are frequently the small change of exchanges in the political community formed by political elites and journalists.

Vertical communication via the media increasingly bypasses official information dissemination. The Stationery Office is the country's largest publisher, and many government departments spend a great deal on diffusion of information about their activities. In 1972 four ministries featured in the list of the top 100 advertisers, and the Central Office of Information itself had an advertising budget four times that of the largest commercial advertiser.[30] Nonetheless the major route of vertical political communication is via the media, and in this politicians have a mechanism whose significance has grown steadily in Britain this century, the lobby. The lobby is part of the parliamentary Press Gallery, and comprises a hundred or more reporters from Press, broadcasting and the news agencies. They are accredited to the lobby and adhere to its rules of conduct. Their task is to attend the routine briefings given by ministers and others, and to report on the political scene within Westminster. Their role in the political system is unique, and has engendered frequent criticism that they are, in one journalist's derisory phrase, 'the messenger boys of British democracy'.[31] The combination of formal rules and informal procedures has lent the lobby an exclusive clublike aura which many have felt blunts the critical element essential in political journalism. The dual communications role of the lobby correspondents has been brought out in research by Tunstall. Their horizontal function, for example, arises because

> seen from one of the less dramatic ministries in Whitehall the lobby correspondents appear as prominent warriors in the political battle who are producing stories that will be on the front pages tomorrow morning, where not only the public but other civil servants, industrial leaders, Cabinet Ministers — and the Prime Minister — will see them.[32]

At the same time they play a key role in vertical

communications, since '. . . the electorate depend to a considerable extent for their political maps upon the lobby ,men'.[33]

Tunstall's study brings out the general interpenetration of journalism and politics, which he found

> is such that some MPs use their seats in Parliament partly as a platform for freelance journalism; the lobby correspondents on the other hand can almost be regarded as co-opted Members of Parliament, whose lack of voting and other rights is balanced by superior access to information and to outlets for publicising their views. Political journalists and politicians also appear to have very similar definitions of news value.[34]

Televising of parliament has been repeatedly proposed to bypass the lobby, but has so far always been rejected.[35]

The horizontal go-between function of political journalism is frequently stressed by its practitioners. John Whale, for example, has written that 'one of the main modern usefulnesses of news organisations is within government . . . the clients whom many journalists have in mind when they write about public affairs are people in the industry of government'.[36] The predominance of horizontal communication may in this way make mass communications less significant than the mass media in the political process. In a study of Glasgow, Budge divided the local political system into three strata of councillors, party workers, and electors. He found that the proportion of current affairs and news television watched increased upwards through the strata, but that political communication was primarily horizontal within the strata. He found no evidence of opinion leaders among the electors.[37]

The complex interaction of the media and the political system needs to be much more thoroughly explored than hitherto, but it is clearly an interrelationship involving considerably more than electoral studies suggest especially in considering the long-term non-purposive role of the media in describing the political process.

THE MEDIA AND OTHER SOCIALISING AGENCIES

Socialising agencies are those social institutions in which people learn about areas of life in which they are not directly involved, and from which they acquire ways of understanding events in their own lives. In the early years the family and school are important; later, work enters more centrally into the socialising process. Friendship patterns and also the media are consistently important, though the media are insufficiently discussed in this context. In this section the role of the media in relation to these other socialising agencies is examined.

Schools

The growth of an industry to cater for teenage leisure has created an image of a homogeneous youth culture and led to discussion of the effects of the media on young people, their attitudes to school life and society in general. For many young people, however, the major media, television and the national Press, are not central in their leisure pursuits. Teenagers watch less television than any other age group, and a great deal of research has demonstrated its limited salience for them. In a study of 600 fourteen-year-old Aberdonians Smith found that only a very small proportion were interested in the media or used them in conversation. When they did turn to the media it was primarily for relief of boredom in the absence of anything better.[38] For these groups the mass media are attended to in terms of their coverage of pop music, fashion and other particular leisure concerns which are catered for more by records, magazines and radio. The bigger pop music magazines have circulations of several hundred thousand, as do the largest teenage weeklies dealing with romance, pop music, and fashion. Among adolescents the most listened to radio station (Radio One), the most frequently watched television programme (*Top of the Pops*), together with the best-selling magazine for teenage girls (*Jackie*) are based either entirely or substantially on developments in pop music and happenings in the pop and fashion worlds.

Much of the research in this field has considered the pop media and school as alternate and competing contenders for young people's attention; it is in this sense that educationalists have spoken about 'education against the environment'. Research by Brown and O'Leary, for example, suggested that 'academic work and pop music were, to some extent at least, alternative foci of interest — and even alternative sources of reputation. Those who failed to shine academically may have turned alternatively to pop music as a source of peer group prestige.'[39] In fact recent research shows the situation to be more complex than this. Murdock and Phelps have described how young people have two alternative sets of activities available outside the school in which to invest the expressive and emotional demands unsatisfied by education.[40] These are the local or 'street' culture of peers, clubs, coffee-bars and makeshift sports, and the media culture of pop. The groups most involved in pop are those middle-class pupils who do not succeed in meeting the academic requirements and expectations attached to them by school and parents, and working-class girls, for whom the alternative culture of sport or street is less available than for boys in the same milieux.

For teachers media output is problematic, and frequently perceived as a threat to traditional curricular values, as well as an inherently undesirable consumer of their pupils' time and interest. Their own exposure to media output is quite different from that of their pupils. In the Murdock and Phelps study teachers read more of the serious press and watched less television than either their pupils or the general population. While almost two-thirds of the youngest (under twenty-five) teachers claimed to listen to pop music at least 'fairly often', overall only 33 per cent of teachers shared this experience with their pupils, and 71 per cent of grammar school teachers claimed they never listened to pop. Murdock and Phelps conclude that 'mass media experiences may tend to aggravate rather than reduce the gaps between teachers and pupils'.[41] English teachers were especially concerned with the harmful impact of media material. While a minority agreed some media output might be stimulating to the imagination, most thought it would more probably be, a deterrent to the acquisition of more conventionally legitimated literacy tastes and skills. Science teachers, more likely to perceive the media as technically interesting in themselves, also commended them for frequently alerting children to wider horizons in science and technology. For this reason media material is seldom introduced into teaching because of its inherent attractions for pupils, but is only used where such material is seen as a useful adjunct and stimulus to the existing, traditional curriculum.[42] McQuail, commenting on the introduction of television into education, has remarked that

it poses a more specific challenge to a predominantly verbal academic tradition and to a formal and systematised approach to teaching . . . there is at least evidence to suggest that most resistence to using television in education comes from those sectors where traditional academic and cultural values are most deeply entrenched.[43]

Peers

As a general source of ideas about the world, friends and associates are an important social group, to whom reference is made for appropriate behaviour and attitudes, and from whom reactions about oneself are received. There are two ways in which the media intervene in these interactions. Firstly, peer groups can associate to use the media which become the focal points around which the groups define themselves. An aspect of peer group use of the media is the adoption of media material as the basis for social interaction among peers, either by providing the leisure activities whose active pursuit knits the peer group together, or in providing information which usefully amplifies the interests of the group. Research by McQuail, Blumler and Brown suggests that the larger the network of acquaintances the more extensive the 'coin of exchange' use of media material will be.[44] The Murdock and Phelps study described earlier also showed how media *styles* can be appropriated by groups of young people as sets of symbols around which to consolidate their groups' identities. Other research has shown the importance of media *information* as a basis of interaction. Eyre-Brook's political socialisation study found that, despite limited interest in the news, 46 per cent of the adolescents she studied talked about the news with friends, though hardly at all with school teachers. In this way selective use of media material is a means of defining appropriate behaviour in different social contexts and groups as well as being a differentiating characteristic of these groups.

The second way in which the media become involved in peer group activities is by themselves becoming notional reference groups. This can occur with fictional material, 'whereby the audience member enters into a vicarious relationship with media personalities . . . as if they could stand in for real persons'.[45] This fairly innocent involvement is more important in the long term in suggesting acceptable ways of social behaviour, and providing cues about social roles and ethics which may be unavailable in the immediate environment, for example about groups with whom personal contact is limited. Hartmann and Husband, in a study of the ways the media interpret and affect race relations, suggest that information is gleaned incidentally, and has led to a predominant definition of immigrants and of immigration as a threat. The media do not directly shape attitudes to immigrants, rather people's attitudes were found to relate to whether they lived in an immigrant area or not, and in turn those attitudes affect the interpretation of media material about immigrants. They conclude that 'the way race-related material is handled by the mass media serves both to perpetuate negative perceptions of blacks and to define the situation as one of inter-group conflict'.[46] In interviews with children Hartmann and Husband found that those who lived in areas of low immigration relied more heavily on the media for information about blacks and were more likely to see their presence as creating conflict. In areas of high immigration personal contacts were, obviously, higher, and personal, affective evaluations of coloured people more positive. However, in response to general questions about the effects of immigration and the nature of immigrant groups, even children with considerable personal knowledge of individual black people volunteered remarks couched in the negative, conflict-oriented frameworks derived from the media.[47]

The family

The media and the family have often been described as competing for children's allegiance, and as making conflicting claims through which the media are eroding parental authority. A common fear has been expressed by Hollander, who claims that 'the new parent is the mass media'.[48] This belief was the centre of widespread concern in the early days of television. A common confusion has been to consider young people's disaffection from family life as the seductive effect of the mass media, while concentrating research and discussion increasingly on television alone. Two research generalisations have calmed much of this particular concern. The first is the limited salience of television for adolescents and its restricted use by them. The second is the recurrent finding that in some senses television 'promotes family life'. Belson, in 1956, found that the introduction of television had increased staying at home in the evenings and by reducing social visits and other leisure pursuits, had encouraged family togetherness, though not in larger families. But he found that 'changes were more in terms of *redistribution* of the time spent at home than alterations in its total quantity'.[49] Himmelweit, whose influential studies on children and television were carried out at much the same point in television history, found that 'children and parents alike try to present television as a beneficial influence on the family'.[50] Her respondents felt that the family with television was at home more, spent more time together, got on better together, and had more in common. However, the study cautions that 'television, although centred on the home, does not greatly strengthen family ties, even though it may offer a spurious sense of unity'.[51]

Differences within the family need to be considered here. Women watch more television than men, for example, and obviously age is a crucial determinant of taste and behaviour. But such differences are less significant than those between families. The much-discussed generation gap may be less fundamental than the differences between families in different locations in the class structure. Thus the modes of expression employed in the search for autonomy from parental authority may well be derived from the media, but will be selected by different young people in different ways in confronting very different sorts of problems. This is quite contrary to the more usual notion that the mass media are making families alike in behaviour and attitudes. Rather it suggests that while differences between groups in society retain their structure and basis, sometimes new symbols are adopted to articulate those differences. Cohen, for example, in a study of London's east end, has written of the different subcultures entered into by adolescents using media-derived styles, as generalisations of intra-family conflicts which are themselves born of the particular situation of working-class families in a changing environment.[52] Similarly, in a study of the television viewing of working-class families in Portsmouth, Piepe and Box described the different viewing habits of what they term the home-centred ('new') working class and the traditional working class. They concluded that 'response to television is selective in terms of the needs and values that audiences bring to their viewing, and the overall picture may be one of growing heterogeneity rather than homogeneity'.[53] This general conclusion belies the idea of the media supplanting parents as socialising agencies, and supports the notion that both are complementary sources of socialisation into the overall social structure.

Work

Work is the major socialising agency of adult life, and is vitally important in the later years of school life as preparation for entry into the labour market becomes a major latent function of education. The nature of people's work shapes the amount and type of leisure they have, while the media provide many of the facilities for using this leisure. The media also play an important role in industrial relations, often, in increasingly large and impersonal organisations, providing much of the general information available to workers and management alike about industry generally and industrial relations in particular. Because of the conventions of journalism and news broadcasting much of what is portrayed of industry concerns the dramatic and overt conflicts of strikes and disputes. Further, because news interests tend to be directed to the effects of strikes — public inconvenience or personal hardship — such presentations can convey a negative evaluation of strikes and, by extension, of trade unions. In Eyre-Brook's study, of those adolescents questioned who relied on the media for their information in this area, nearly two-thirds thought it was wrong that people are allowed to go on strike. In an analysis of the way the media portrayed industrial strife in the 1970 dock strike one sociologist concluded that 'the focus was always on the negative implications rather than on its causes even in current affairs items'.[54]

As yet there have been no major long-term studies of this kind. Short-term studies often concentrate, predictably, on the grievances of offended parties or interest groups. One media union, the ACTT, has conducted a study of television coverage of one week's activities in industrial relations. Their reading of the output led them to claim that 'industrial matters are covered in an erratic and superficial way'. The union's Television Commission deplored the lack of background information and investigation, and, referring to BBC reporting of one strike, felt that 'the absence of views from the people involved, the use of loaded language . . . and the failure to discuss the background issues was nothing short of scandalous'.[55] Aims of Industry, a free enterprise pressure group, has also done monitoring in this way, and publishes a monthly *Report on Television and Industry* which comments on what it feels to be unfair representation of business interests. Both viewpoints reflect a growth in coverage of industry.

> Trouble at the mill is no longer a subject of merely local gossip. It is often a national story. Trouble in the boardroom is no longer merely a delicious tit-bit for the stock exchange and the clubs. The protagonists may find themselves in a cockfight on '24 Hours' or 'This Week'.[56]

One result of such coverage is the entry of media imagery of disputes into the perceptions of people involved in negotiations. Lane and Roberts, in a case study of a strike in St Helens, noticed this happening at two levels. The emphasis given to the small amount of violent picketing 'presented an image of no little chaos and of personal risk to those who had

97

returned to work'.[57] On another level the authors note that those they call 'the generals', the strike leaders and union officials embroiled in the dispute, read Press reports, especially lengthy features, in a more involved manner. Such material 'helped them to clarify many of their own ideas, it provided them with some sort of framework into which they could fit many of their own experiences'.[58] A more detailed study of the use of the media by union leaders has been conducted by Blumler and Ewbank.[59] They found that involvement in union affairs decreased the likelihood of acceptance of media images of industry. After correlating media use with opinions about industry they found

> some support . . . for the proposition that concern about the unofficial strike problem varies inversely with the likelihood of experiencing it directly. It can also be seen that the influence of the broadcasting variables remained significant, even after the impact of all the other variables had been taken into account.

Blumler and Ewbank's findings suggested that the Press had little influence on unionists' views about unofficial strikes, but that radio and television had played a 'slight but significant part' in generating concern. However, union officials were unaffected by media presentation.

Of course media impact on work socialisation will not be entirely on attitudes to industrial relations. But since this is the most salient aspect of media coverage of work it is likely to dominate such effects as the media do have. More general considerations, for example the extent to which fictional presentation of occupational roles has an effect on job aspirations, await extensive research in this country. It is likely that in this area, as with other complementary sources of socialisation, attitudes *to* the immediate situation are based on factors *in* the immediate situation (school, housing, friends, parents, workplace), whereas broader attitudes to general social issues will be shaped much more by the media.

THE MEDIA AND CULTURAL VALUES

As influential purveyors of public information and providers of leisure facilities the media industries have a profound effect on people's values and beliefs. Traditionally two distinct analyses of the impact of the media after industrialisation have described such effects. Critics of the right have accused the media of spreading cultural material of little worth to an uncritical populace, negating the beneficial effects of mass education and pandering to the lowest common cultural denominators in the search for commercial success. The cure should be a return to the security of tried central values of excellence, controlled by paternalistic guardianship of the production of culture. This view, thematically consistent through the writings of educationalists and cultural critics like Mathew Arnold, T. S. Eliot, F. R. Leavis, and G. Steiner, has seen the popular media as threats to traditional culture from which stern criticism must rescue lost standards and embattled values. Opponents of this view stigmatise it as elitist and reactionary, and deny that the values being eroded are any more central or vital than those of media culture, or that they ever were indeed so central as their defenders claim.

The contrary analysis, from the left, attacks the media for their trivialised and distorted portrayal of working-class life; for their manipulative use by power-holding elites either to distract the working class from its revolutionary potential or to persuade it that it has none; and for their role in spreading values in support of an inegalitarian *status quo* by presentation and legitimation of a political consensus. Latterly the growth of advertising-based media has added the further accusation that in diffusing values of conspicuous consumption or 'consumerism' the media induce economic behaviour which supports and is consistent with the same political consensus they sustain in these other ways. Opponents of this view say it is but another form of elitism, an intellectualised misreading of working-class reality which

99

neglects the radical tradition in journalism, and which contains a strong air of patronising the working-class victims it aspires to protect.

In this debate about 'mass culture', a third strand has often emerged which seeks to assert a different kind of critical appraisal by deciding what is valid or worthwhile in any level of cultural product rather than by discerning high or low standards of intrinsic excellence. Richard Hoggart is closely associated with this line of argument, and has suggested that 'this is to make distinctions between the quality of life in each thing of its own kind'.[60] This way of thinking is an attempt to erase notions of the relative merit of 'brow-levels', but often becomes totally non-sociological in treating cultural products as disembodied and rootless materials for analysis according to uncodifiable criteria of validity.

The media have been held to change values in particular areas of social life by presenting as normal behaviour that is not, or by exposing the innocent and vulnerable to disturbing and distorted displays of the less pleasant aspects of social reality. Recent research by Croll has suggested that such concern may be self-creating, in that expressions of anxiety represent awareness that the issue is part of public discussion rather than deriving from deliberate and personal consideration of the media's harmful effects. The conclusion of this research was that

> absence of convincing research findings linking violence or declining moral standards with television or other media, suggests that public concern about these links may be better regarded as an expression of a diffuse social anxiety than as rational beliefs about the influence of the media.[61]

While, for example, only between 6 and 12 per cent of Croll's respondents mentioned excessive sex or violence as areas of concern in television output, 36 per cent agreed there was cause for anxiety about these topics when they were suggested to them.

In another piece of research the same author has looked at the role of the media in influencing views about crime. A content analysis of crime reports in newspapers showed that violent crimes and crimes whose newsworthiness lay in the human interest aspects of their victims were over-reported in comparison with their frequency in official crime statistics. A survey of readers found them to be particularly concerned about violent attacks, especially on the old and other defenceless people.

> The replies showed no awareness of the extent to which violent crime takes place between people who know each other, and are even members of the same family ... Mentioning violent crime was found to be related to the extent to which the respondent read the local newspaper, and the extent to which he relied on it for crime news.[62]

The media, then, are shaping values about social acts they portray, and in a more circular fashion about the culture they themselves manufacture and disperse. In a preliminary report of research on film censorship Guy Phelps has argued that not merely attitudes to the cinema but also public authority control of films are the result of discussions of films in the other media. Changing cinema ethics, he suggests, serve as easily identifiable and censurable moral objects in a situation where the more complex fragmenting moral consensus of the wider society is beyond the purview of the news media.[63] The debate about sex and violence in the cinema and on television has been endless. On the one hand, for example, the media have been accused of destroying necessary inhibitions and inciting imitative hooliganism and 'permissiveness'. On the other hand critics have attacked television especially for upholding traditional middle-class family life styles against the reality of changing relations between the sexes, and for ignoring the intrinsic violence of oppression and political agencies of control while glamourising the meaningless violence of private eyes and jet set intrigue. These conflicting assessments have usefully switched the debate to the long-term contribution of the media to cultural values, and away from the immediate impact of individual media products on isolated acts, about which research is inconclusive and likely to remain so.

THE MEDIA AND THE SOCIAL SYSTEM

This chapter has looked at a variety of institutions with which the media interact. The media are involved in the social system in four ways apart from their importance as leisure and entertainment industries. They are actors in other institutions, in political and industrial life, for example. They are communicators explaining institutions to the people involved in them by both vertical and horizontal communication. They are information brokers, conveying messages in and through social processes, and, finally, they are legitimators of values and institutions in the public arena, conferring status and validity, and setting the agenda for political and cultural debate.

A main theme in these processes is the reconciliation that often needs to be made between the information and values people derive from direct personal experience and those they receive from the media. It is fair to hypothesise that the media play their most significant role in imparting values in areas of comparative abstractness, distance, unfamiliarity and inaccessibility, while behaviour in and attitudes about personally experienced circumstances are more directly the result of the situation surrounding these circumstances. All generalisations about the media and the social system must have regard to changes in each, and the next chapter is concerned with the changing nature of the mass media themselves.

The changing media 6

TECHNOLOGY AND ORGANISATION

Changes in the media industries have always been stimulated by technical developments and new means of mass communication. The diode valve, cinema sound, the steam printing press, telegraphy, the transistor, paperback book-binding and so on have all facilitated major changes in the nature of the media and the forms of communications available. Some writers, most popularly and eccentrically Marshall McLuhan, have seen such changes as the key determining factor in the effects of the media, and indeed as conditioning a wide variety of social processes. In the scheme of Chapter 2 these changes are an important part of the supply side of the communications equation.

Many of the recent technical innovations in communications have generated a euphoria about the new possibilities they could open up in ways of moving information or serving new leisure patterns. These hopes should be set against organisational inertia, which may colonise new technologies for existing needs and contents. To a considerable extent the major media companies have already incorporated the new technologies into their present activities. Groups controlling the record market have captured the cassette industry. Those in film production have quickly coalesced video hardware, and newspapers and television companies have staked their claim in local radio as rapidly as other media organisations have moved into cable television. Consequently a tension has developed between the possibilities suggested by the new technology for different sorts of social organisation in the media on the one hand, and the conventional uses to which the innovations have been put on the other. This chapter describes the major changes in the media in the light of this general relationship between technology and organisation.

BROADCASTING

Television has become the main medium for most people in Britain, and, since the transistor, radio has discovered new audiences and maintained an important place in the technology of entertainment. In recent years there have been a number of calls for a resurgence of local broadcasting, the form in fact in which the BBC began its life. The BBC experimented with closed circuit local radio broadcasts in 1958–59, but the Pilkington Committee, reporting in 1962, saw 'little evidence of significant, spontaneous public demand', although it did think the experiments justified 'a sustained and broadly-based trial, in the expectation than an extensive pattern of local stations might follow'.[1] Stations in Leicester, Sheffield, and on Merseyside opened in 1967, in a further five cities in 1968, and in another twelve during the following three years. By 1971 local radio was available to 74 per cent of the population.

In many cases the areas served by local radio stations were large conurbations rather than communities in any sociological sense. Research conducted during the first two years of local radio by Wells and West showed that, initially, at least two-thirds of the population made little or no use of the new medium. This was in part due to the limited ownership of VHF radio sets, but also symptomatic of a lack of real interest. This research report, commenting on the limited impact of local radio at this stage, suggests 'this may be a reflection of the fact that local radio seems to appeal most to those for whom a concern for and willingness to participate in local affairs is already strongly developed, rather than to those whose interest on *a priori* grounds, might need to be cultivated'.[2] The authors found, further, that local radio played little part in increasing communication between local groups, though it did serve a self-consciously useful function in crises and disasters. Coverage of local government activities, however, did not seem to stimulate interest or involvement in them.

Use of local radio output was mixed. The main reason for regular listening was to hear news programmes; two-thirds of those who listened at all made a routine of listening to news broadcasts. While 45 per cent of listeners claimed to have learnt a fair amount, or even a great deal about their locality from local radio, council activities and local events were low among the particular matters they had in mind. As for stimulating new involvements, 'it would not appear that local radio has stimulated many to do what they would not already have done in its absence'.[3] Participation in community affairs was little advanced by local radio.

In general the report notes the general lack of success of local radio in terms of its declared community aims, which seems to have led to a decreasing reference to these initial aims in later evaluations of local radio's potential. In 1973 the first five contracts for commercial local radio stations were granted, two for London, one each for Manchester, Birmingham and Glasgow. It is too early to estimate to what extent any declared aims of community enhancement will be met, nor whether the necessity for these aspirations to be reconciled with commercial viability will prove intractable. However, the preliminary research on non-commercial local radio is not promising.

Local television has been available technically for many years. Cable, or 'community-antenna' television, feeding signals directly to domestic receivers, has been widely used in areas where local topography has made reception inadequate. Potentially the cable can convey up to forty channels, including locally originated programmes, and it is these latter possibilities that have provoked speculation about the radical alterations in the organisation of broadcasting which might ensue from the wider introduction of cable TV. An even more radical possibility derives from the possibility of 'feedback', that is, of communication from viewers to the cable centre or even multilaterally. Here the social demand for greater audience participation and active criticism is latent in the technology itself. The first station offering locally originated programmes opened in south-east London in 1972, and four more were licensed to open in 1973. Further government decisions about broadcasting have been postponed and any major changes in the 1970s will be made in the knowledge that a large-scale re-evaluation of broadcasting is likely in a few years' time. The only imminent decision relates to the allocation of the fourth channel.

A second technical development in television is in new forms of storage of recorded visual material available for home reproduction, including magnetic videotape, laser holograms on vinyl, PVC discs, electronically processed films, and so on. As with cable the new technology has provoked interest in its social ramifications, in this case the increased opportunity for viewers to choose when and what they watch. However, many doubts remain about the realisation of these hopes. Firstly, commercial companies have already established extensive ownership of the new devices, and American experience suggests that their use will be predominantly restricted to contents of established popularity and marketability.[4] The large-scale manufacture needed to make these products economically worth while has directed their use to popular entertainments, pornography, and educational materials.

Much of the debate about the future of broadcasting has paid scant attention to the present demands and attitudes of viewers, or to their opinions about possible futures for the broadcast media. Recent research has uncovered public knowledge and attitudes on these issues.[5] Most people demand changes and make criticisms entirely in terms of programming and scheduling; in the Leicester survey only 1 per cent of respondents mentioned changes in structure or control, or improvements in access or public participation. Local television was the most popular choice for a fourth channel from a series of alternative uses suggested to respondents, but did not capture an overwhelming vote, and a larger proportion opted for extension of something resembling the existing services. The comment of the earlier Pilkington Committee is apposite: 'If people do not know what they are missing they cannot be said not to want it.' In response to questions about their demands for future broadcasting people inevitably lean towards the familiar, or reformulations of it.

The third important change in broadcasting is the rapid evolution of international communications. For radio this is already commonplace. Television viewers are increasingly accustomed to the arrival of television programmes by satellite, and from other countries in Europe via the Eurovision circuit. News programmes have been in the forefront of European and intercontinental transmissions for some time, and within Eurovision British broadcasting organisations play a leading role, reflecting the early growth of British broadcasting, the centrality of London as a news and telecommunications route focus, and the magnitude of the BBC and ITV networks. For example, in the first half of 1971, of the 1,809 news items exchanged through the Eurovision news circuit, 29 per cent came from the BBC and a further 20 per cent from Independent Television News.

Satellite transmissions have been increasingly used in recent years since the launching of a series of satellites in the 'INTELSAT' system.[6] The significant development of direct transmission to individual receivers, however, remains an expensive possibility. Even within the existing possibilities for international news exchanges in both Eurovision and via satellites three limitations remain. First, the flow has continued to be mainly *from* the news capitals *to* the newly accessible areas of the developing world. Second, as far as satellites are concerned, television material comprises only a very small fraction of the traffic they carry and is extremely expensive to obtain in this way. Third, the use of Eurovision for programme exchanges other than news is dominated by sport, which in 1972 provided 78 per cent of such material compared with 13 per cent of current affairs and similar programmes.[7]

Generally then, broadcasting technology promises two contrasting evolutions, localisation and internationalisation. But the mere existence of technical facilities is no guarantee of their being used in novel or socially original ways.

THE PRESS

The recent past and prospects of the British Press are normally discussed in an air of gloom and crisis, several of the reasons for which were outlined in Chapter 2. Yet there are a series of imminent changes which could sustain optimism. James Curran has argued that, contrary to most views, newspaper consumption has increased overall due to a smaller number of newspapers actually producing more pages.[8] Ailing national dailies survive with perennial transfusions from the industrial combines which own them, and much of the provincial Press is not just subsisting but indeed expanding.

After the economic changes described in Chapter 2 had weeded the provincial Press, consolidation into groups (by 1972 five chains controlled 40 per cent of the morning and 59 per cent of the evening circulations), and expansion of classified local advertising kept this sector buoyant into the 1970s. The circulation of provincial morning newspapers increased by over 10 per cent between 1962 and 1972. However, a continuing decline in the number of provincial papers, the rapid rise in costs, and development of local commercial radio and shopper 'give-aways' as competitors for advertising all make the welfare of the local Press difficult to predict.

The problems of serving real communities and at the same time meeting the demands of commercial survival are parallel to those of local radio. Many provincial newspapers sell to the majority of households in their area, and one study of the role of these weeklies saw them as 'a more intimate form of communication to the reader who is an active participant in community life'.[9] In general, however, Jackson notes that in the provincial Press the extensive coverage of non-local crime, especially in the dailies, and the timorous, even platitudinous approach to local politics, prevent the full realisation of this potential. Cox and Morgan, in a study of the local Press in Liverpool, found deficiencies in local political journalism in five of the six papers they considered. 'The problem was less that important issues were shirked, than that it seemed almost impossible to impart a large amount of information without being either too detailed or too dull for all but the most avid of readers.'[10] These researchers note the emergence of cheaply produced local newspapers in Liverpool as one response to these inadequacies. One of their six traditional newspapers was much like these in style and readership,

> having as constituency not a whole town or city but only a particular section of it both socially and geographically . . . it was freer than others to concentrate on covering a smaller range of issues affecting that section — the south Liverpool working-class — who were its main readers.[11]

Community-based small circulation newspapers, often relying on volunteer sales forces and non-profit-making printers, have emerged in many British cities in recent years, though often selling as much to younger transient sections of the population as to long-established local residents. More overtly political than the 'underground' or 'countercultural'

Press, these papers have nonetheless attracted less attention than the more ostentatiously outrageous of the latter.

As with broadcasting, technological changes in the Press promise social effects, particularly in the direction of localised and cheaper production. Web-offset printing, and computer and photographic typesetting could facilitate decentralised printing. The ultimate development, frequently predicted, is the 'telenewspaper', with facsimiles printed in the home from local printing and telegraphic typesetting centres.[1][2] Also like broadcasting, the twin social possibilities of consumer selection — of those sections of the available signal wanted in printed form for retention — and local community orientation, are seen as inherent in the new technology.

However, as one senior proprietor has put it, 'the chilling fact is that survival of newspapers depends not on their social utility but on their ability to command advertising'.[1][3] The ability to command advertising requires large circulations, or at least a circulation amongst groups attractive to advertisers by virtue of their wealth and status, or special interest in a particular range of products. A local working-class area, for example, would exhibit none of these characteristics. The media are competing for advertising expenditure which has not grown as quickly as gross national product for a number of years. The share of advertising going to national newspapers has declined from 19.8 per cent in 1960 to 18.4 per cent in 1972; in the same period the proportion going to television has increased from 22.3 per cent to 24.9 per cent. In possibly conceding news coverage increasingly to broadcasting the popular Press may become steadily more like entertainment-oriented daily magazines. Public trust of the news media already favours the broadcast media. In a survey in 1972, 63 per cent of respondents named television or radio as their most important source of news against 28 per cent who opted for newspapers, and when asked to name which medium they would believe if given different accounts of a news story, 68 per cent chose television, while only 18 per cent chose newspapers.[14] The implications for the changing nature and use of newspapers remain unclear but are likely to be reflected in any changes prompted by technical developments. Any future increase in colour printing in national newspapers, for example, may advance their similarity to magazines because of the need to pre-prepare colour printing, limiting its use to features rather than news.

CINEMA

A victim of changing leisure patterns, the cinema has been pronounced dead with morbid regularity ever since the decline in attendances was first noticed. But, as with the other media, embers of optimism have been fanned by recent organisational changes which it is hoped may herald a new character and function for the industry. Two major chains dominate film exhibition, owning roughly a third of the cinemas between them and a much higher proportion of the plusher profitable city-centre houses. One and a half thousand cinemas closed between 1960 and 1970, but in the 1970s there have been some indications that the fall in attendances at the remaining cinemas is levelling off. While the absolute number of admissions fell by roughly two-thirds between 1960 and 1971, the ratio of admissions per cinema only dropped by about 26 per cent in the same period. However, this is scant comfort in the face of a continuing decline in cinema attendance. It is given a happier tinge by evidence which suggests that 'there has been an upsurge in the number of cinema-goers. This amounts in absolute terms to 17 per cent' between 1961 and 1971.[15] In other words more people are going to the cinema, but on average are doing so less frequently.

Further signs of revitalisation are seen in the number of smaller, twin or multiple cinemas which have opened in recent years. There were thirty-nine of these in 1969, and 144 by 1972. This has led one analyst to argue that 'small cinemas, without charging too much, attract the greatest numbers of people relative to the local potential'.[16] The growth of cinema clubs and institutes, though often pornography-based, is also a result of a renewed interest in cinema, especially among the younger audiences who form the bulk of film-goers. Over half the cinema audience is under twenty-four years old, and optimists have suggested that this may signal a resurgence in cinema-going as a leisure habit, a hope that has been realised to a degree in the United States and Italy, though there is no convincing evidence yet in Britain. The construction of smaller cinemas implies the same redifferentiation of supply as seems inherent in the technological changes in the other media discussed earlier. Yet at the same time consolidation in production may be reducing the choice of films offered. After the nadir of 1969–70, American film production companies have recovered on the crest of the wave created by the demands of television and their involvement in other diversified activities. Television series frequently spawn successful feature films and the two industries are now closely entwined. Four of the twenty most successful films of 1972 were adapted from television comedy series, while between fifteen and twenty feature films are shown on television in an average week.

One stage back in the film supply chain production itself has shown signs of becoming increasingly redifferentiated. The proportion of British films made by independent producers increased from 16 per cent in 1968 to 36 per cent in 1972.[17] However, film exhibition remains very largely in the hands of two chains, while in 1972 three chains distributed sixteen of the top twenty films. Small-scale production exploiting cheap cameras and new editing and processing techniques would seen unlikely to make a significant difference to the cinema in the light of these organisational constants.

PUBLISHING

The problems of publishing were outlined in Chapter 2. They have frequently moved observers to predict the death of the book, or at least of the novel, under the onslaught of the electronic media and what are seen as the seductive attractions of newer, less demanding activities. This essentially patrician viewpoint is not strictly in accord with the evidence. Book prices have indeed massively increased as the costs of printing, binding, and paper have spiralled. The index of book prices used by libraries rose by 112 per cent between 1965 and 1971. Nonetheless the number of titles has continued to proliferate, from 23,783 in 1960 to 35,254 in 1973. The rising value of book sales reflects rising prices and the development of exports rather than a real growth in domestic consumption, but the domestic sales of educational paperbacks alone doubled from 1969 to 1972, and in the same three years the revenue from all book sales in Britain increased by 43 per cent.

The growth of educational publishing and of paperbacks has maintained the rise in book buying, but overall the rapid rise in prices has kept the rate of increase of total consumer expenditure on books since 1961 down to less than 2 per cent per year at constant prices. The arrival, and indeed predominance of the paperback has not only altered the character of publishing but has kept book purchasing alive despite the gloomy prognostications of its demise. Most reading, however, is of borrowed books. The massive growth of library use mentioned in Chapter 2 contradicts the patterns of book buying. A survey in 1966, for example, found that 73 per cent named a novel as the last book they had read.[18]

The responses in publishing to cost and other pressures have already been described, in particular the financial importance of paperbacks and the penetration of multimedia firms into the industry. But concurrently there has been an increase in the number of smaller publishers. The total number of publishers increased from 1,054 in 1950 to 1,766 in 1973. While large publishers concentrate on the major growth areas in educational publishing, popular fiction, children's books and so on, smaller publishers have increasingly catered for minority interests, and over 1,500 of these publishers issue less than fifty titles each per year. Pressures for commercial novelty within publishing have produced the coffee-table book and part works, but also new cheaper forms of printing which have been enthusiastically exploited by smaller independent publishers. On the whole, however, successful publishing requires a scale of production, distribution and promotion beyond the resources of the smaller publishers.

In all the media, then, new techniques in production or distribution hold the promise of redefining their social use. Increased local or community media, wider choice with the corollary of accommodating minority requirements, 'feedback', cheap production, internationalisation, and so on, all appear among the possibilities facilitated by technical innovation. The extent to which economics and organisational arrangements will accept and encourage these changes is yet to be seen, but will serve as a reminder of the total immersion of changes in the media in other societal processes.

CHANGING MEDIA AND CHANGING SOCIETY

Throughout this book we have seen how the mass media are intimately involved in a variety of social processes. Far from being separate social institutions which can be examined in a conceptual vacuum, the media are inextricably part, by virtue of what they are and what they produce, of every important social institution. Yet, as the gaps in this account will amply have illustrated, we know not nearly enough about the internal functions and external effects of the media, not least because of the recurrent misconceptions surrounding these questions.

114

The limited perspective which treats the media as isolated from other organisations and processes in society is only one blinker, however; the other is provided by the mistake of seeing the media in modern Britain as being of only domestic concern. In Chapter 3 some of the international ramifications of current reorganisation in the media were described. Of course, problems like the allocation of a fourth television channel, the changing character of the BBC, the crises in Fleet Street and so on have their specifically British aspects. But the modern media are no longer solely national any more than the problems that beset them or the societies they serve. The development of international companies and media markets, technological expansion, the spread of ideas, examples, and personnel, all contribute if not to a 'global village', at least to a necessary awareness that no medium is a purely local phenomenon. Study of the British media is illuminating because of their historically important role in the spread of mass communications in other areas, not only in imperial territories. It is illuminating, too, because Britain still has one of the highest consumptions of media material of any nation. Compared with the United Nations minimum standards of ten daily newspapers, five radios, two cinema seats and two televisions for every hundred inhabitants, Britain is a communications cornucopia. The operations, effects, and problems of the British media are exemplary as important instances of mass communications in any advanced industrial society. It should no longer be possible to consider significant changes in these societies without appreciation of the role of communications and of the media in providing for so many of the ideas, values, and changing patterns of behaviour with which sociology is concerned.

References and further reading

CHAPTER 1 THE MASS MEDIA AND SOCIAL SCIENCE

1. D. Horton, *Television's Story and Challenge*. Harrap, 1951, p. 11.
2. See D. Thompson, *Voice of Civilisation*, Muller, 1943.
3. D. Thompson, Foreword to F. Inglis, *The Imagery of Power*, Heinemann, 1972.
4. See, for example, some of the contributions to a symposium edited for the National Union of Teachers by B. Groombridge; *Popular Culture and Personal Responsibility*, NUT, 1961.
5. F. C. Wertham, *Seduction of the Innocent*, Rinehart, 1954.
6. J. J. Tobias, *Crime and Industrial Society in the Nineteenth Century*, Penguin edition, Penguin Books, 1972, pp. 98—9.
7. M. Whitehouse, *Cleaning Up TV*, Blandford Press, 1967.
8. J. C. W. Reith, quoted in A. Briggs, *The Birth of Broadcasting*, Oxford University Press, 1961, p. 244.
9. J. Agassi, 'The worker and the media', *Archives Européennes de Sociologie*, 11 (1970), pp. 26—66.
10. Wordsworth's Preface of 1800, in Wordsworth and Coleridge, *Lyrical Ballads*, Oxford University Press, 1911, pp. 230—1.
11. F. Williams, *Dangerous Estate*, Arrow Books, 1959, p. 81.
12. J. C. Stobart, quoted in A. Briggs, *The Golden Age of Wireless*, Oxford University Press, 1965, p. 261.
13. H. T. Himmelweit, A. N. Oppenheim, P. Vince, *Television and the Child*, Oxford University Press, 1958.
14. For reviews of these developments in Britain see J. D. Halloran, *The Effects of Mass Communication*, Leicester University Press, 1965, and the same author's Introduction to J. D. Halloran, ed., *The Effects of Television*, Panther Books, 1970.

15. See D. McQuail *Towards a Sociology of Mass Communications,* Collier-Macmillan, 1969.
16. For accessible sources see B. P. Emmett, 'The television and radio audience in Britain', in D. McQuail, ed., *Sociology of Mass Communications,* Penguin Books, 1972, pp. 195—219, and brief overviews in the annual HMSO publication *Social Trends.*
17. See C. Seymour-Ure, *The Press, Politics, and the Public,* Methuen, 1968, ch. 2.
18. *National Readership Survey,* Jan.-Dec. 1973, published by the Joint Industrial Committee for National Readership Surveys (JICNARS).
19. Screen Advertising Association, *Facts about the Cinema,* 1972. The ratios mentioned were calculated by the author from Department of Trade and Industry figures for 1971 as 3.7 for Scotland, 3.1 for the South-West, 1.7 for the South-East, and 1.6 for the GLC London area.
20. European Research Consultants, *Report on Books and Reading Habits,* 1965.
21. P. Worsley, 'Libraries and mass culture', in *Library Association Record,* August 1967.
22. See the review of research in P. Mann, *Books, Buyers and Borrowers,* Deutsch, 1971.
23. D. McQuail, J. Blumler, and J. Brown, 'The television audience: a revised perspective', in McQuail, ed. *op. cit.*
24. For a discussion of this type of research as conducted by the BBC see B. P. Emmett, 'A new role for research in broadcasting', *The Public Opinion Quarterly,* 33, no. 4 (1968—69), pp. 654—65.
25. D. C. Chaney, 'Television dependency and family relationships amongst juvenile delinquents in the United Kingdom', *The Sociological Review,* 18, no. 1 (1970), pp. 103—13.
26. J. D. Halloran, R. L. Brown, and D. Chaney, *Television and Delinquency,* Leicester University Press, 1970.
27. *Future of Broadcasting, Preliminary Report,* Centre for Mass Communication Research, University of Leicester, Feb. 1973 (mimeo).

117

CHAPTER 2 THE HISTORY AND DEVELOPMENT OF THE MEDIA IN BRITAIN

1. M. L. DeFleur, 'Mass communications and social change', *Social Forces,* 44 (1966), pp. 314–26.
2. See summary figures in *Social Trends,* HMSO (annual).
3. The figures in this paragraph and in Table 1 are approximate due to various deficiencies in official sources. Table 1 is derived from the 1972 *Family Expenditure Survey,* Department of Employment, HMSO, 1973. The average expenditure figure is based on preliminary figures from the 1971 census and figures collated from the *Annual Abstract of Statistics.* All calculations are the author's. The categories used are such as to make generalisations difficult, and those figures should be treated with some caution.
4. G. Murdock and G. Phelps, 'Youth culture and the school revisited', *British Journal of Sociology,* 23, no. 4 (Dec. 1972), pp. 478–82.
5. S. H. Steinberg, *Five Hundred Years of Printing,* New York, Criterion Books, 1959, p. 75.
6. I. Watt, *The Rise of the Novel,* London, Peregrine Books, 1962, ch. 2.
7. L. Stone, 'Literacy in England 1640–1900', *Past and Present,* February 1969.
8. Quoted in C. Hill, *The Century of Revolution, 1603–1714,* London, Sphere Books, 1969, p. 232.
9. R. D. Altick, *The English Common Reader,* University of Chicago Press, 1963, p. 37.
10. Quoted in *ibid.,* p. 275.
11. See R. Collison, *The Story of Street Literature,* Dent, 1973.
12. M. Deane, 'United Kingdom publishing statistics', *Journal of the Royal Statistical Society,* Series A, 1951, pp. 468–89.
13. IPC, *Report on a Small Study of the Reading of Books,* 1965.

14. Research on the audience for books is limited and confused. For an important recent contribution and summary of earlier work see P. H. Mann and J. L. Burgoyne, *Books and Reading*, Deutsch, 1969; and P. Mann, *Books: Buyers and Borrowers*, Deutsch, 1971.

15. See R. Astbury, *Libraries and the Book Trade*, London, Clive Bingley, 1968.

16. Figures in these sections calculated by the author from a variety of sources.

17. F. Williams, *Dangerous Estate, the anatomy of newspapers* (Longmans, 1957) inclines to this style but remains the standard general history.

18. C. King, *The Future of the Press*, MacGibbon and Kee, 1967.

19. See R. M. Wiles, *Freshest Advices; early provincial newspapers in England.* Ohio University Press, 1965.

20. See P. Pinkus, *Grub Street Stripped Bare*, Constable, 1968.

21. Among numerous accounts see J. Pendleton, *Newspaper Reporting in Olden Times and Today*, London, Elliot Stock, 1890.

22. See F. S. Siebert, *Freedom of the Press in England, 1476–1776*, University of Illinois Press, 1965, ch. 17. Macaulay's famous remarks were made in 1834.

23. A. Aspinall, 'The circulation of newspapers in the early nineteenth century', *Review of English Studies* (1946), pp. 29–43.

24. For the importance of the agencies at this time see P. Elliott and P. Golding, 'The news media and foreign affairs', in R. Boardman and A. Groom, eds., *The Management of Britain's External Relations*, Macmillan, 1973, pp. 305–30.

25. R. Williams, *The Long Revolution*, Penguin Books, 1965, p. 219.

26. P. Ferris, *The House of Northcliffe*, Weidenfeld and Nicolson, 1971.

27. I am indebted to unpublished research by James Curran for these figures.

28. For the relevant figures see A. P. Wadsworth, 'Newspaper circulations 1800—1954', *Manchester Statistical Society,* 1955.
29. R. Low and R. Manvell, *The History of the British Film 1896—1906,* Allen & Unwin, 1948.
30, R. Low, *The History of the British Film 1906—1914,* Allen & Unwin, 1949.
31. A. Briggs, *Mass Entertainment: the origins of a modern industry,* Adelaide University Press, 1960.
32. R. Low, *The History of the British Film 1918—1929,* Allen & Unwin, 1971.
33. See Cinematograph Films Act 1927, HMSO, 17 & 18. Geo. V.
34. See A. Wood, *Mr. Rank: a study of J. Arthur Rank and British films,* Hodder & Stoughton, 1952.
35. J. Spraos, *The Decline of the Cinema,* Allen & Unwin, 1962.
36. I. Montagu, *Film World,* Penguin Books, 1964, p. 221.
37. See review by J. Terry, 'The future of the British film industry, *Screen,* 11, no. 4/5 (1970), pp. 115—28.
38. *National Film Finance Corporation Annual Report, 1971,* HMSO, Sess. 1970—71, Cmnd 4761. para. 13.
39. T. Kelly *et al, A Competitive Cinema,* London, Institute of Economic Affairs, 1966, p. 44.
40. See T. Guback, *The International Film Industry, Western Europe and America since 1945,* Indiana University Press, 1969.
41. National Film Finance Corporation, *Annual Report, 1972,* HMSO, Cmnd 5080, 1971—72, p. 4.
42. J. C. W. Reith, *Into the Wind,* Hodder & Stoughton, 1949, pp. 90—1.
43. A. Briggs, *The Birth of Broadcasting,* Oxford University Press, 1961, pp. 235—9.
44. *ibid.,* p. 401.
45. See G. R. M. Garratt and A. H. Mumford, 'The history of television', *Proceedings of the Institution of Electrical Engineers,* 99 (1952), part IIIA, pp. 25—42.
46. H. H. Wilson, *Pressure Group,* Secker & Warburg, 1961. This is the best account of the political campaign for ITV.

47. See P. Masson, 'The effects of television on the media', in J. D. Halloran, ed., *The Effects of Television,* Panther, 1970, pp. 138–80.
48. See National Board for Prices and Incomes Report No. 156, *Costs and Revenues of Independent Television Companies,* HMSO, Cmnd 4524, 1970.

CHAPTER 3 THE STRUCTURE AND ORGANISATION OF THE MEDIA

1. For an elaboration of this point see G. Murdock and P. Golding, 'The political economy of mass communications', in R. Miliband and J. Saville, eds., *Socialist Register, 1973,* London, Merlin Press, 1974.
2. In fact for 1973–74 total expenditure on external broadcasting will be £17 million, a little under half the total government expenditure on overseas information: see *Supply Estimates 1973–74,* HMSO, Cmnd 5248, Sess. 1972–73, Table IX.
3. For a general description see M. Ogilvy-Webb, *The Government Explains,* Allen & Unwin, 1965.
4. For a full discussion of this system see the *Second Report from the Select Committee on Nationalised Industries: The Independent Broadcasting Authority,* HMSO, 1972, H. C. Paper 465. Sess. 1971–72.
5. I am grateful to Guy Phelps for help with this section: see his research in G. Phelps, *Censorship and the Cinema,* in preparation.
6. F. Williams, *The Right to Know,* Longman, 1969, p. 277.
7. Chairman's Foreword to the 1972 Press Council Annual Report; *The Press and The People,* London, Press Council, 1972.
8. See R. J. Glessing, *The Underground Press in America,* Indiana University Press, 1971 and for a British comparison, R. Lewis, *Outlaws of America,* Penguin Books, 1972.
9. Central Statistical Office, *National Income and Expenditure,* HMSO, 1972, Table 22.

10. R. A. Critchley, *U.K. Advertising Statistics,* London, The Advertising Association, 1973, Tables 1 and 3.
11. *ibid.,* adapted from Table 7; 1972 figures taken from *Advertising Quarterly,* Summer 1973.
12. Stuart Hood, *The Mass Media,* Macmillan, 1972, p. 91.
13. See G. Matthews, 'Freedom for whom?' in E. Moonman, ed., *The Press: a case for commitment,* Fabian Tract 391, London, The Fabian Society, 1969, esp. p. 19.
14. Murdock and Golding, *op. cit.* adapted; see the article for elaboration and sources of statistics.
15. *ibid.* Figures are approximate in some instances due to varying categorisation.
16. T. Varis, *International Inventory of Television Programme Structure and the Flow of TV Programmes Between Nations.* Research Institute, University of Tampere, 1973, pp. 205—10.
17. See C. F. Pratten, *The Economics of Television,* London, PEP Broadsheet 520, 1970.
18. J. S. Mill, 'On Liberty', in J. S. Mill; *Utilitarianism, Liberty, and Representative Government,* Dent, Everyman Library, 1910, p. 79.
19. See S. Hood, 'Creativity and accountancy', in E. G. Wedell, ed., *Structures of Broadcasting,* Manchester University Press, 1970.

CHAPTER 4 THE COMMUNICATORS AND MEDIA PRODUCTION

1. M. Bradbury, *The Social Context of Modern English Literature,* Blackwell, 1971, part three.
2. R. Findlater, *The Book Writers: who are they?* London, The Society of Authors, 1966, see updated figures by Findlater in *The Author,* Winter, 1972.
3. J. Tunstall, *Journalists at Work,* Constable, 1971, pp. 136—7.
4. D. F. Laurenson, 'A sociological study of authorship', *British Journal of Sociology,* 20, no. 3 (Sept. 1969), pp. 311—25.

5. R. D. Altick, 'The sociology of authorship', *New York Public Library Bulletin,* 66, no. 6 (June 1962), pp. 389–404; see also R. Williams, *The Long Revolution,* Penguin Books, 1965, pp. 254–70.
6. Tunstall, *op. cit.,* p. 96.
7. O. Boyd-Barrett, 'Journalism recruitment and training: problems in professionalisation', in J. Tunstall, ed., *Media Sociology,* Constable, 1970, p. 187.
8. *ibid.,* p. 190.
9. *BBC Handbook,* 1973, p. 195.
10. Boyd-Barrett, *op. cit.* p. 192.
11. National Board for Prices and Incomes, Report 115, *Journalists' Pay,* HMSO 1969, Cmnd 4077, Table 6.
12. Tunstall, *Journalists at Work,* p. 63.
13. Estimated from A. Roth and J. Kerby, *The Business Background of M.P.s.* London, Parliamentary Profile Services Ltd, 1972.
14. T. Burns, 'Commitment and career in the BBC', in D. McQuail, ed., *Sociology of Mass Communications,* Penguin Books, 1972, p. 290.
15. As described in A. Jay, *Public Words and Private Words,* London, Society of Film and Television Arts, 1972.
16. See P. Elliott, *The Making of a Television Series,* Constable, 1972, pp. 126–34.
17. M. Lane, 'Publishing managers, publishing house organisation, and role conflict', *Sociology,* 4 (1970), p. 369.
18. I. C. Jarvie, *Towards a Sociology of the Cinema,* Routledge and Kegan Paul, p. 55.
19. I. Montagu, *Film World,* Penguin Books, 1964, p. 211.
20. Huw Weldon, quoted in *Taste and Standards in B.B.C. Programmes,* BBC, 1973, p. 11.
21. S. Hood, *A Survey of Television,* Heinemann, 1967, p. 50.
22. Royal Commission on the Press. *Minutes of Oral Evidence, vol. I,* HMSO, 1962, Cmnd 1812, pp. 188–93.
23. Elliott, *op. cit..* p. 146.

24. For a more extended treatment see G. Murdock and P. Golding, 'The political economy of mass communications', in R. Miliband and J. Savile, eds, *Socialist Register, 1973,* London, Merlin Press, 1974.
25. C. Wintour, *Pressures on the Press,* Deutsch, 1972, p. 3.
26. A. M. Carr-Saunders and P. Wilson, *The Professions,* Oxford University Press, 1933, p. 270.
27. Burns, *op. cit.*. p. 293.
28. Bradbury, *op. cit.,* pp. 122—8.
29. J. D. Halloran *et al., Demonstrations and Communication: a case study,* Penguin Books, 1970.
30. Tunstall, *op. cit.,* p. 233.
31. Elliott, *op. cit.,* p. 135.
32. D. McQuail, 'Uncertainty about the audience and the organisation of mass communications', in *The Sociological Review: Monograph no. 13,* Keele, 1969, pp. 75—84.
33. Elliott, *op. cit.,* p. 139.
34. T. Burns, 'Public service and private world', in *The Sociological Review, Monograph no. 13,* p. 70.
35. J. Blumler, 'Producers' Attitudes towards Television Coverage of an Election Campaign: A Case Study,' in *The Sociological Review, Monograph no. 13,* p. 90.
36. Elliott, *op. cit.,* p. 106.
37. Television Research Committee, *Second Progress Report and Recommendations,* Leicester University Press, 1969, p. 28.
38. McQuail, *op. cit.,* p. 82.
39. Burns, 1969, *op. cit.,* p. 64.
40. *ibid.,* p. 72
41. Elliott, *op. cit.,* pp. 141—2.
42. Tunstall, *op. cit.,* p. 252.
43. S. Hood, *op cit.,* p.38—9.
44. A. Mitchell, 'The decline of current affairs television', *Political Quarterly,* Summer 1973, pp. 127—36.
45. G. Noble, 'Report of the "Blue Peter" project', in P. Taff, ed., *Report on the First E.B.U. Workshop for Producers of Children's Television Programmes,* Geneva, European Broadcasting Union, 1969, pp. 118—33.

46. Tunstall, *op. cit.*, p. 258.
47. Lane, *op. cit.*, p. 371.
48. Carr-Saunders and Wilson, *op. cit.*, p. 267.
49. F. J. Mansfield, *Gentlemen, The Press*, W. H. Allen, 1943.
50. See *The Report of the Broadcasting Committee, 1949*, HMSO, 1951, Cmnd 8116, ch. 18.
51. For details of this dispute and other information, see *The Select Committee on Nationalised Industries: Report on the Independent Broadcasting Authority*, HMSO, 1972, H. C. 465. Sess. 1971–72, pp. 139–53.

CHAPTER 5 THE MEDIA AND THE SOCIAL SYSTEM

1. Sir Robert Fraser, 'The troubles of democracy', (lecture reprinted from 1969) in K. J. McGarry, ed., *Mass Communications*, London, Clive Bingley, 1972, p. 212.
2. For American research see K. and G. Lang, *Politics and Television*, Chicago, Quadrangle Books, 1970. The major British study is J. D. Halloran *et al., Demonstrations and Communication: A case study*, Penguin Books, 1970.
3. J. Trenaman and D. McQuail, *Television and the Political Image*, Methuen, 1961, p. 173.
4. J. G. Blumler and D. McQuail, *Television in Politics: Its Uses and Influence*, Faber, 1968, p. 215.
5. H. G. Nicholas, *The British General Election of 1950*, Macmillan, 1951, ch. 6.
6. See D. E. Butler, *The British General Election 1951*, Macmillan, 1952.
7. D. E. Butler and R. Rose, *The British General Election of 1959*, Macmillan, 1960.
8. M. Harrison, 'Television and radio', in D. E. Butler and A. King, *The British General Election of 1964*, Macmillan, 1965.
9. Blumler and McQuail, *op. cit.*, p. 218.
10. D. Butler and D. Stokes, *Political Change in Britain*, Penguin Books, 1971, p. 299.
11. Blumler and McQuail, *op. cit.*, pp. 64–77.
12. *ibid.*, chs. 11 and 13.
13. Nicholas, *op. cit.*, ch. 6.

14. *ibid.*, ch. 7.
15. J. G. Blumler, 'The political effects of television', in J. D. Halloran, ed., *The Effects of Television*, Panther, 1970, p. 77.
16. M. Harrison, chapters on broadcasting in D. E. Butler and A. King, *The British General Election of 1966*, Macmillan, 1966; and D. Butler and M. Pinto-Duschinsky, *The British General Election of 1970*, Macmillan, 1971.
17. Blumler, *op. cit.*, p. 84.
18. The two-step flow theories are to be found in P. F. Lazarsfeld, *et al.*, *The People's Choice*, New York, Duell, Sloan and Pearce, 1944; E. Katz and P. F. Lazarsfeld; *Personal Influence*, Free Press of Glencoe, 1955; and in E. Katz; 'the two step flow of communications: an up-to-date report on a hypothesis', *Public Opinion Quarterly* (1957), pp. 61—78.
19. Butler and Stokes, *op. cit.*, p. 266.
20. See U. Kitzinger, *Diplomacy and Persuasion*, Thames & Hudson, 1973, chs. 11 and 12.
21 E. Eyre-Brook, 'Political socialisation and the mass media', unpublished thesis, Leicester, Centre for Mass Communication Research, 1973.
22. H. T. Himmelweit, *et al.*, *Television and the Child*, Oxford University Press, 1958, pp. 254—5.
23. N. Johnson, 'Children's Comics', *New Society, 8*, (1966) no. 197, pp. 7—12.
24. A. Morrison and D. McIntyre, *Schools and Socialisation*, Penguin Books, 1971, p. 153.
25. C. Seymour-Ure, *The Press, Politics, and the Public*, Methuen, 1968, p. 266.
26. A. Barker and M. Rush, *The M.P. and His Information*, Allen & Unwin, 1970, pp. 39—49.
27. *The Report of the Review Committee on Overseas Representation, 1968—69*, HMSO, 1969, Cmnd 4107, see also P. Elliott and P. Golding, 'The news media and foreign affairs' in R. Boardman and A. Groom, The *Management of Britain's External Relations*, Macmillan, 1973.

28. Seymour-Ure, *op. cit.*, p. 266–76.

29. *ibid.*, pp. 289–300.

30. The author's figures. For a descriptive account see M. Ogilvie-Webb; *The Government Explains*, Allen & Unwin, 1965.

31. Anthony Howard, quoted in J. Tunstall, *The Westminster Lobby Correspondents*, Routledge & Kegan Paul, 1970, p. 21, see also Seymour-Ure, *op. cit.*, pp. 198–240.

32. Tunstall, *op. cit.*, p. 63.

33. *ibid.*, p. 95.

34. *ibid.*, p. 98.

35. For an extensive discussion see C. Wilson, ed., *Parliament and its Means of Contact with Public Opinion through the Radio, Press, and Television*, Geneva, the Interparliamentary Union, 1968, (London, Cassell 1970).

36. J. Whale, *Journalism and Government*, Macmillan, 1972, p. 29.

37. I. Budge, *et al.*, *Political Stratification and Democracy*, Macmillan, 1972.

38. D. M. Smith, 'Some uses of mass media by 14-year olds', *Journal of Broadcasting*, 16, no. 1 (Winter 1971–72), pp. 37–50.

39. R. L. Brown and M. O'Leary, 'Pop music in an English secondary school system', in *American Behavioral Scientist*, 14, no. 3, 1971, p. 412.

40. G. Murdock and G. Phelps, *Mass Media and the Secondary School*, Macmillan Education, 1973. This section is heavily indebted to their research report.

41. *ibid.* p. 9.

42. *ibid.*, ch. 3.

43. D. McQuail, 'Television and education', in J. D. Halloran, ed., (1970) *op. cit.*, p. 193.

44. D. McQuail, J. Blumler and J. Brown, 'The television audience: a revised perspective' in D. McQuail, *Sociology of Mass Communication*, Penguin Books, 1972, pp. 135–65.

45. *ibid.*, p. 157.

46. P. Hartmann and C. Husband, 'The Mass Media and Racial Conflict', *Race*, 12 (1970–71), p. 270.

47. See the full report in P. Hartmann and C. Husband, *Racism and the Mass Media*, London, Davis-Poynter, 1973.
48. N. Hollander, 'Adolescence and War; the source of Socialisation', unpublished paper presented at Conference of International Association of Mass Communication Research, Konstanz, 1970.
49. W. A. Belson, *The Impact of Television*, Crosby Lockwood, 1967, p. 313.
50. H. T. Himmelweit *et al.*, *Television and the Child*, Oxford University Press, 1958, p. 379. The research was conducted in 1955—56.
51. *ibid.*, p. 383.
52. P. Cohen, 'Subcultural conflict and working-class community', *Working Papers in Cultural Studies*, no. 2, Spring 1972; pp. 5—51, University of Birmingham.
53. A. Piepe and A. Box, 'Television and the new working class', *New Society*, 21, no. 521, 28 September 1972. pp. 606—8.
54. J. Downing, 'Class and "Race" in the British News Media', unpublished paper, 1971.
55. A.C.T.T. Television Commission, *One Week*, ACTT, London, 1971, p. 10.
56. C. H. King, *Industry and Mass Communication*, The Industrial, Educational and Research Foundation, London, 1968, p. 11.
57. T. Lane and K. Roberts, *Strike at Pilkingtons*, Fontana, 1971, p. 78.
58. *ibid.*, p. 82.
59. J. G. Blumler and A. J. Ewbank, 'Trade unionists, the mass media and unofficial strikes', *British Journal of Industrial Relations*, 1970, pp. 32—54.
60. R. Hoggart, 'Culture: dead and alive', reprinted in the same author's *Speaking to Each Other*, Penguin, 1973, Vol. 1, pp. 129—32.
61. P. Croll, 'The nature of public concern with television with particular reference to violence', in J. D. Halloran and P. Croll, *Violence and the Media*, Davis-Poynter, forthcoming.

62. In, *ibid.* P. Croll, 'Crime reporting and public beliefs about deviant behaviour'.
63. G. Phelps, 'Censorship and the Press,' *Sight and Sound,* 42, no. 3, Summer, 1973, pp. 138–40.

CHAPTER 6 THE CHANGING MEDIA

1. *Report of the Committee on Broadcasting, 1960,* HMSO, 1962, Cmnd 1753, Memorandum II, p. 1044.
2. A. Wells and J. West, *Local Radio and the Community,* mimeo, Mass Communication Research Centre, Leicester, 1971, p. 219.
3. *ibid.,* p. 186.
4. See C. Christians, 'Home video systems: a revolution?' *Journal of Broadcasting,* (17, no. 2, Spring 1973, pp. 223–31.
5. Centre for Mass Communication Research, *Future of Broadcasting – Preliminary Report,* Leicester CMCR, February 1973, (mimeo).
6 See, *inter alia,* A. Chayes *et al., Satellite Broadcasting,* Oxford University Press, 1973, and B. Maddox; *Beyond Babel,* André Deutsch, 1972. Part II.
7. Statistical summary in *EBU Review,* 24, no. 3, May 1973, Geneva, European Broadcasting Union, p. 45.
8. J. Curran, 'The impact of television on the audience for national newspapers 1945–68', in J. Tunstall, ed., *Media Sociology,* Constable, 1970, pp. 104–31.
9. I. Jackson, *The Provincial Press and the Community,* Manchester University Press, 1971, p. 273.
10. H. Cox and D. Morgan, *City Politics and the Press,* Cambridge University Press, 1973, p. 132.
11. *ibid.,* p. 134.
12. See M. Granek; 'Technical developments for the newspaper industry', in *The Penrose Annual, 1972,* Lund Humphries, London, 1972.
13. C. King, 'The Press, the public, and the future', in *The Future of the Press,* McGibbon & Kee, London, 1967, p. 115.

14. Centre for Mass Communication Research, *Future of Broadcasting, preliminary report, op. cit.*
15. M. Shaw 'Alice in Wonderland', *Journal of the Market Research Society,* 15 no. 1, 1973, pp. 52—5.
16. C. H. B. Williamson, 'What the figures mean', *Cinema TV Today,* 6 Jan 1973. pp. 38—9.
17. Based on figures in *ibid.,* p. 30.
18. See the summary in P. Mann, *Books: Buyers and Borrowers,* Deutsch, 1971.

Index